The
C
Answer
Book

The
C
Answer
Book

Second Edition

Solutions to the Exercises in
The C Programming Language, Second Edition
by Brian W. Kernighan and Dennis M. Ritchie

Clovis L. Tondo
International Business Machines Corporation

Scott E. Gimpel

PRENTICE HALL, Englewood Cliffs, New Jersey 07632

Library of Congress Cataloging-in-Publication Data

Tondo, Clovis L.
  The C answer book : solutions to the exercises in The C
programming language, second edition, by Brian W. Kernighan and
Dennis M. Ritchie / Clovis L. Tondo, Scott E. Gimpel.—2nd ed.
    p.   cm.—(Prentice Hall software series)
  Includes index.
  ISBN 0-13-109653-2
    1. C (Computer program language)—Problems, exercises, etc.
I. Gimpel, Scott E.   II. Kernighan, Brian W.   C programming
language.   III. Title.   IV. Series.
QA76.73.C15K47 1988 suppl.
005.13′3—dc19   88-25134
                                                       CIP

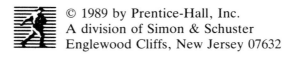

© 1989 by Prentice-Hall, Inc.
A division of Simon & Schuster
Englewood Cliffs, New Jersey 07632

Prentice Hall Software Series
Brian Kernighan, Advisor

UNIX is a registered trademark of AT&T.

Printed in the United States of America
10 9 8 7 6 5 4 3 2

ISBN 0-13-109653-2

Prentice-Hall International (UK) Limited, *London*
Prentice-Hall of Australia Pty. Limited, *Sydney*
Prentice-Hall Canada Inc., *Toronto*
Prentice-Hall Hispanoamericana, S.A., *Mexico*
Prentice-Hall of India Private Limited, *New Delhi*
Prentice-Hall of Japan, Inc., *Tokyo*
Simon & Schuster Asia Pte. Ltd., *Singapore*
Editora Prentice-Hall do Brasil, Ltda., *Rio de Janeiro*

Contents

Preface

This is an ANSWER BOOK. It provides solutions to all the exercises in *The C Programming Language*, second edition, by Brian W. Kernighan and Dennis M. Ritchie (Prentice Hall, 1988)*.

The American National Standards Institute (ANSI) produced the ANSI standard for C and K&R modified the first edition of *The C Programming Language*. We have rewritten the solutions to conform to both the ANSI standard and the second edition of K&R.

Careful study of *The C Answer Book*, second edition, used in conjunction with K&R, will help you understand C and teach you good C programming skills. Use K&R to learn C, work the exercises, then study the solutions presented here. We built our solutions using the language constructions known at the time the exercises appear in K&R. The intent is to follow the pace of K&R. Later, when you learn more about the C language, you will be able to provide possibly better solutions. For example, until the statement

```
if (expression)
        statement-1
else
        statement-2
```

is explained on page 21 of K&R, we do not use it. However, you could improve the solutions to Exercises 1-8, 1-9, and 1-10 (page 20 K&R) by using it. At times we also present unconstrained solutions.

We explain the solutions. We presume you have read the material in K&R up to the exercise. We try not to repeat K&R, but describe the highlights of each solution.

You cannot learn a programming language by only reading the language constructions. It also requires programming—writing your own code and study-

---

*Hereafter referred to as K&R.

ing that of others. We use good features of the language, modularize our code, make extensive use of library routines, and format our programs to help you see the logical flow. We hope this book helps you become proficient in C.

We thank the friends that helped us to produce this second edition: Brian Kernighan, Don Kostuch, Bruce Leung, Steve Mackey, Joan Magrabi, Julia Mistrello, Rosemary Morrissey, Andrew Nathanson, Sophie Papanikolaou, Dave Perlin, Carlos Tondo, John Wait, and Eden Yount.

Clovis L. Tondo

The
C
Answer
Book

CHAPTER 1

A Tutorial Introduction

Exercise 1-1: (page 8 K&R)

Run the "hello, world" program on your system.   Experiment with leaving out parts of the program to see what error messages you get.

```
#include   <stdio.h>

main()
{
      printf("hello, world");
}
```

In this example the newline character (\n) is missing.   This leaves the cursor at the end of the line.

```
#include <stdio.h>

main()
{
      printf("hello, world\n")
}
```

In the second example the semicolon is missing after printf().   Individual C statements are terminated by semicolons (page 10 K&R).   The compiler should recognize that the semicolon is missing and print the appropriate message.

```
#include <stdio.h>

main()
{
      printf("hello, world\n');
}
```

In the third example the double quote " after \n is mistyped as a single quote. The single quote, along with the right parenthesis and the semicolon, is taken as part of the string.   The compiler should recognize this as an error and complain that a double quote is missing, that a right parenthesis is missing before a right brace, the string is too long, or that there is a newline character in a string.

Exercise 1-2: (page 8 K&R)

Experiment to find out what happens when printf's argument string contains
\c, where c is some character not listed above.

```
#include <stdio.h>

main()
{
      printf("hello, world\y");
      printf("hello, world\7");
      printf("hello, world\?");
}
```

The Reference Manual (Appendix A, page 193 K&R) states

If the character following the \ is not one of those specified, the behavior
is undefined.

The result of this experiment is compiler dependent.   One possible result might
be

```
hello, worldyhello, world<BELL>hello, world?
```

where <BELL> is a short beep produced by ASCII 7. It is possible to have a
\ followed by up to three octal digits (page 37 K&R) to represent a character.
\7 is specified to be a short beep in the ASCII character set.

Exercise 1-3: (page 13 K&R)

Modify the temperature conversion program to print a heading above the table.

```
#include <stdio.h>

/* print Fahrenheit-Celsius table
    for fahr = 0, 20, . . ., 300; floating-point version */
main()
{
    float fahr, celsius;
    int lower, upper, step;

    lower = 0;   /* lower limit of temperature table   */
    upper = 300; /* upper limit                        */
    step  = 20;  /* step size                          */

    printf("Fahr Celsius\n");
    fahr = lower;
    while (fahr <= upper) {
        celsius = (5.0/9.0) * (fahr-32.0);
        printf("%3.0f   %6.1f\n", fahr, celsius);
        fahr = fahr + step;
    }
}
```

The addition of

```
printf("Fahr Celsius\n");
```

before the loop produces a heading above the appropriate columns. We also added two spaces between %3.0f and %6.1f to align the output with the heading. The remainder of the program is the same as on page 12 K&R.

Exercise 1-4: (page 13 K&R)

Write a program to print the corresponding Celsius to Fahrenheit table.

```
#include <stdio.h>

/* print Celsius-Fahrenheit table
    for celsius = 0, 20, ..., 300; floating-point version  */
main()
{
    float fahr, celsius;
    int lower, upper, step;

    lower = 0;          /* lower limit of temperature table */
    upper = 300;        /* upper limit                      */
    step  = 20;         /* step size                        */

    printf("Celsius  Fahr\n");
    celsius = lower;
    while (celsius <= upper) {
        fahr = (9.0*celsius) / 5.0 + 32.0;
        printf("%3.0f  %6.1f\n", celsius, fahr);
        celsius = celsius + step;
    }
}
```

The program produces a table containing temperatures in degrees Celsius (0–300) and their equivalent Fahrenheit values. Degrees Fahrenheit are calculated using the statement:

```
fahr = (9.0*celsius) / 5.0 + 32.0
```

The solution follows the same logic as used in the program that prints the Fahrenheit-Celsius table (page 12 K&R). The integer variables lower, upper, and step refer to the lower limit, upper limit, and step size of the variable celsius, respectively. The variable celsius is initialized to the lower limit, and inside the while loop the equivalent Fahrenheit temperature is calculated. The program prints Celsius and Fahrenheit and increments the variable celsius by the step size. The while loop repeats until the variable celsius exceeds its upper limit.

Exercise 1-5: (page 14 K&R)

Modify the temperature conversion program to print the table in reverse order, that is, from 300 degrees to 0.

```
#include <stdio.h>

/* print Fahrenheit-Celsius table in reverse order           */
main()
{
     int fahr;

     for (fahr = 300; fahr >= 0; fahr = fahr - 20)
          printf("%3d %6.1f\n", fahr, (5.0/9.0)*(fahr-32));
}
```

The only modification is:

```
for (fahr = 300; fahr >= 0; fahr = fahr - 20)
```

The first part of the for statement,

```
fahr = 300
```

initializes the Fahrenheit variable (fahr) to its upper limit.   The second part, or the condition that controls the for loop,

```
fahr >= 0
```

tests whether the Fahrenheit variable exceeds or meets its lower limit.   The for loop continues as long as the statement is true.   The step expression,

```
fahr = fahr - 20
```

decrements the Fahrenheit variable by the step size.

Exercise 1-6: (page 17 K&R)

Verify that the expression `getchar() != EOF` is 0 or 1.

```
#include <stdio.h>

main()
{
    int c;

    while (c = getchar() != EOF)
        printf("%d\n", c);
    printf("%d - at EOF\n", c);
}
```

The expression

```
c = getchar() != EOF
```

is equivalent to

```
c = (getchar() != EOF)
```

(page 17 K&R). The program reads characters from the standard input and uses the expression above. While `getchar` has a character to read it does not return the end of file and

```
getchar() != EOF
```

is true. So 1 is assigned to `c`. When the program encounters the end of file, the expression is false. Then 0 is assigned to `c` and the loop terminates.

Exercise 1-7: (page 17 K&R)

Write a program to print the value of EOF.

```
#include <stdio.h>

main()
{
    printf("EOF is %d\n", EOF);
}
```

The symbolic constant EOF is defined in <stdio.h>. The EOF outside the double quotes in printf() is replaced by whatever text follows

```
#define EOF
```

in the include file. In our system EOF is -1, but it may vary from system to system. That's why standard symbolic constants like EOF help make your program portable.

Exercise 1-8: (page 20 K&R)

Write a program to count blanks, tabs, and newlines.

```
#include <stdio.h>

/* count blanks, tabs, and newlines                          */
main()
{
    int c, nb, nt, nl;

    nb = 0;                           /* number of blanks     */
    nt = 0;                           /* number of tabs       */
    nl = 0;                           /* number of newlines   */
    while ((c = getchar()) !=EOF) {
        if (c == ' ')
            ++nb;
        if (c == '\t')
            ++nt;
        if (c == '\n')
            ++nl;
    }
    printf("%d %d %d\n", nb, nt, nl);
}
```

The integer variables nb, nt, and nl are used to count the number of blanks, tabs, and newlines, respectively.   Initially, these three variables are set equal to 0.

Inside the body of the while loop, the occurrence of each blank, tab, and newline from input is recorded.   All if statements are executed each time through the loop. If the character received is anything but a blank, tab, or newline, then no action is taken.   If it is one of these three, then the appropriate counter is incremented.   The program prints the results when the while loop terminates (getchar returns EOF).

The if-else statement is not presented until page 21 K&R. With that knowledge the solution could be:

```
#include <stdio.h>

/* count blanks, tabs, and newlines                              */
main()
{
    int c, nb, nt, nl;

    nb = 0;                          /* number of blanks        */
    nt = 0;                          /* number of tabs          */
    nl = 0;                          /* number of newlines      */
    while ((c = getchar()) !=EOF)
        if (c == ' ')
            ++nb;
        else if (c == '\t')
            ++nt;
        else if (c == '\n')
            ++nl;
    printf("%d %d %d\n", nb, nt, nl);
}
```

Exercise 1-9: (page 20 K&R)

Write a program to copy its input to its output, replacing each string of one or more blanks by a single blank.

```
#include <stdio.h>

#define NONBLANK 'a'

/* replace string of blanks with a single blank              */
main()
{
    int c, lastc;

    lastc = NONBLANK;
    while ((c = getchar()) != EOF) {
        if (c != ' ')
            putchar(c);
        if (c == ' ')
            if (lastc != ' ')
                putchar(c);
        lastc = c;
    }
}
```

The integer variable c records the ASCII value of the present character received from input and lastc records the ASCII value of the previous character. The symbolic constant NONBLANK initializes lastc to an arbitrary nonblank character.

The first if statement in the body of the while loop handles the occurrence of nonblanks—it prints them. The second if statement handles blanks, and the third if statement tests for a single blank or the first blank of a string of blanks. Finally, lastc is updated, and the process repeats.

The `if-else` statement is not presented until page 21 K&R. With that knowledge the solution could be:

```
#include <stdio.h>

#define  NONBLANK 'a'

/* replace string of blanks with a single blank          */
main()
{
    int c, lastc;

    lastc = NONBLANK;
    while ((c = getchar()) != EOF) {
        if (c != ' ')
            putchar(c);
        else if (lastc != ' ')
            putchar(c);
        lastc = c;
    }
}
```

The logical OR (¦¦) operator is also not presented until page 21 K&R. With that knowledge the solution could be:

```
#include <stdio.h>

#define  NONBLANK 'a'

/* replace string of blanks with a single blank          */
main()
{
    int c, lastc;

    lastc = NONBLANK;
    while ((c = getchar()) != EOF) {
        if (c != ' ' ¦¦ lastc != ' ')
            putchar(c);
        lastc = c;
    }
}
```

Exercise 1-10: (page 20 K&R)

Write a program to copy its input to its output, replacing each tab by \t, each backspace by \b, and each backslash by \\. This makes tabs and backspaces visible in an unambiguous way.

```
#include <stdio.h>

/* replace tabs and backspaces with visible characters      */
main()
{
    int c;

    while ((c = getchar()) != EOF) {
        if (c == '\t')
            printf("\\t");
        if (c == '\b')
            printf("\\b");
        if (c == '\\')
            printf("\\\\");
        if (c != '\b')
            if (c != '\t')
                if (c != '\\')
                    putchar(c);
    }
}
```

The character received from input can be a tab, a backspace, a backslash, or anything else. If it is a tab we replace it with \t, a backspace with \b, and a backslash with \\. Anything else is printed as is.

A backslash character is represented as '\\' in C. We print two backslashes by passing the string "\\\\" to printf.

The `if-else` statement is not presented until page 21 K&R. With that knowledge the solution could be:

```c
#include <stdio.h>

/* replace tabs and backspaces with visible characters     */
main()
{
    int c;

    while ((c = getchar()) !=EOF)
        if (c == '\t')
            printf("\\t");
        else if (c == '\b')
            printf("\\b");
        else if (c == '\\')
            printf("\\\\");
        else
            putchar(c);
}
```

Exercise 1-11: (page 21 K&R)

How would you test the word count program?   What kinds of input are most likely to uncover bugs if there are any?

To test the word count program first try no input.   The output should be: 0 0 0 (zero newlines, zero words, zero characters).
Then try a one-character word.   The output should be: 1 1 2 (one newline, one word, two characters—a letter followed by a newline character).
Then try a two-character word.   The output should be: 1 1 3 (one newline, one word, three characters—two characters followed by a newline character).
In addition, try 2 one-character words (the output should be: 1 2 4) and 2 one-character words—one word per line (the output should be 2 2 4).
The kinds of input most likely to uncover bugs are those that test boundary conditions.   Some boundaries are:

    —no input
    —no words—just newlines
    —no words—just blanks, tabs, and newlines
    —one word per line—no blanks and tabs
    —word starting at the beginning of the line
    —word starting after some blanks

Exercise 1-12: (page 21 K&R)

Write a program that prints its input one word per line.

```
#include <stdio.h>

#define IN   1          /* inside a word                      */
#define OUT  0          /* outside a word                     */

/* print input one word per line                              */
main()
{
    int c, state;

    state = OUT;
    while ((c = getchar()) != EOF) {
        if (c == ' ' || c == '\n' || c == '\t') {
            if (state == IN) {
                putchar('\n');       /* finish the word    */
                state = OUT;
            }
        } else if (state == OUT) {
            state = IN;              /* beginning of word  */
            putchar(c);
        } else                       /* inside a word      */
            putchar(c);
    }
}
```

state is an integer boolean that records whether the program is currently inside a word or not. At the beginning of the program, state is initialized to OUT, since no data has been processed.

The first if statement

```
if (c == ' ' || c == '\n' || c == '\t')
```

determines whether c is a word separator. If it is, then the second if statement,

```
if (state == IN)
```

determines whether this word separator signifies the end of a word. If so, a newline is printed and state is updated; otherwise no action is taken.

If c is not a word separator, then it is either the first character of a word or another character within the word. If it is the beginning of a new word, then the program updates state. In either case, the character is printed.

Exercise 1-13: (page 24 K&R)

Write a program to print a histogram of the lengths of words in its input.   It is
easy to draw the histogram with the bars horizontal; a vertical orientation is
more challenging.

```c
#include <stdio.h>

#define   MAXHIST 15            /* max length of histogram   */
#define   MAXWORD 11            /* max length of a word      */
#define   IN      1            /* inside a word             */
#define   OUT     0            /* outside a word            */

/* print horizontal histogram                                */
main()
{
    int c, i, nc, state;
    int len;                    /* length of each bar        */
    int maxvalue;               /* maximum value for wl[]     */
    int ovflow;                 /* number of overflow words  */
    int wl[MAXWORD];            /* word length counters      */

    state = OUT;
    nc = 0;                     /* number of chars in a word */
    ovflow = 0;                 /* number of words >= MAXWORD*/
    for (i = 0; i < MAXWORD; ++i)
        wl[i] = 0;
    while ((c = getchar ()) != EOF) {
        if (c == ' ' || c == '\n' || c == '\t') {
            state = OUT;
            if (nc > 0)
                if (nc < MAXWORD)
                    ++wl[nc];
                else
                    ++ovflow;
            nc = 0;
        } else if (state == OUT) {
            state = IN;
            nc = 1;             /* beginning of a new word   */
        } else
            ++nc;               /* inside a word             */
    }
    maxvalue = 0;
    for (i = 1; i < MAXWORD; ++i)
        if (wl[i] > maxvalue)
            maxvalue = wl[i];
```

```
for (i = 1; i < MAXWORD; ++i) {
    printf("%5d - %5d : ", i, wl[i]);
    if (wl[i] > 0) {
        if ((len = wl[i] * MAXHIST / maxvalue) <= 0)
            len = 1;
    } else
        len = 0;
    while (len > 0) {
        putchar ('*');
        --len;
    }
    putchar('\n');
}
if (ovflow > 0)
    printf("There are %d words >= %d\n", ovflow, MAXWORD);
}
```

A blank, newline, or tab marks the end of a word. If there is a word (nc > 0) and its length is less than the maximum word length (nc < MAXWORD), then the program increments the appropriate word length counter (++wl[nc]). If the length of the word is out of range (nc >= MAXWORD), then the program increments the variable ovflow that keeps track of the number of words greater than or equal to MAXWORD.

When all words have been read in, the program determines the maximum value (maxvalue) from the array wl.

The variable len scales the value in wl[i] according to MAXHIST and maxvalue. When wl[i] is greater than 0, at least one asterisk is printed.

```
#include <stdio.h>

#define   MAXHIST   15        /* max length of histogram   */
#define   MAXWORD   11        /* max length of a word      */
#define   IN        1         /* inside a word             */
#define   OUT       0         /* outside a word            */

/* print vertical histogram                                */
main()
{
    int c, i, j, nc, state;
    int maxvalue;             /* maximum value for wl[]     */
    int ovflow;               /* number of overflow words   */
    int wl[MAXWORD];          /* word length counters       */
```

```
            state = OUT;
            nc = 0;                      /* number of chars in a word    */
            ovflow = 0;                  /* number of words >= MAXWORD    */
            for (i = 0; i < MAXWORD; ++i)
                wl[i] = 0;
            while ((c = getchar()) != EOF) {
                if (c == ' ' || c == '\n' || c == '\t') {
                    state = OUT;
                    if (nc > 0)
                        if (nc < MAXWORD)
                            ++wl[nc];
                        else
                            ++ovflow;
                    nc = 0;
                } else if (state == OUT) {
                    state = IN;
                    nc = 1;       /* beginning of a new word    */
                } else
                    ++nc;         /* inside a word              */
            }
        maxvalue = 0;
        for (i = 1; i < MAXWORD; ++i)
            if (wl[i] > maxvalue)
                maxvalue = wl[i];

        for (i = MAXHIST; i > 0; --i) {
            for (j = 1; j < MAXWORD; ++j)
                if (wl[j] * MAXHIST / maxvalue >= i)
                    printf(" * ");
                else
                    printf("   ");
            putchar('\n');
        }
        for (i = 1; i < MAXWORD; ++i)
            printf("%4d ", i);
        putchar('\n');
        for (i = 1; i < MAXWORD; ++i)
            printf("%4d ", wl[i]);
        putchar('\n');
        if (ovflow > 0)
            printf("There are %d words >= %d\n", ovflow, MAXWORD);
}
```

This solution prints a vertical histogram. It is similar to the previous program
until maxvalue is determined. Then it is necessary to scale each element of
the array wl and verify whether an asterisk should be printed for each one of
the elements. This verification is necessary since all bars are printed simulta-
neously (vertical histogram). The last two for loops print the index and value
for each element of wl.

Exercise 1-14: (page 24 K&R)

Write a program to print a histogram of the frequencies of different characters
in its input.

```
#include <stdio.h>
#include <ctype.h>

#define MAXHIST 15              /* max length of histogram    */
#define MAXCHAR 128             /* max different characters   */

/* print horizontal histogram freq. of different characters */
main()
{
    int c, i;
    int len;                    /* length of each bar         */
    int maxvalue;               /* maximum value for cc[]      */
    int cc[MAXCHAR];            /* character counters          */

    for (i = 0; i < MAXCHAR; ++i)
        cc[i] = 0;
    while ((c = getchar()) != EOF)
        if (c < MAXCHAR)
            ++cc[c];
    maxvalue = 0;
    for (i = 1; i < MAXCHAR; ++i)
        if (cc[i] > maxvalue)
            maxvalue = cc[i];

    for (i = 1; i < MAXCHAR; ++i) {
        if (isprint(i))
            printf("%5d - %c - %5d : ", i, i, cc[i]);
        else
            printf("%5d -   - %5d : ", i, cc[i]);
        if (cc[i] > 0) {
            if ((len = cc[i] * MAXHIST / maxvalue) <= 0)
                len = 1;
        } else
            len = 0;
        while (len > 0) {
            putchar('*');
            --len;
        }
        putchar('\n');
    }
}
```

This program is similar to the horizontal histogram in Exercise 1-13. Now we are counting the frequency of different characters. We use an array character counter of MAXCHAR entries and we ignore characters greater than or equal to MAXCHAR if they exist in the character set being used. The other difference is that we use a macro to determine if a character is printable. The include file <ctype.h> is discussed on page 43 K&R. isprint is described on page 249 K&R (Appendix B: Standard Library).

Exercise 1-15: (page 27 K&R)

Rewrite the temperature conversion program of Section 1.2 to use a function for conversion.

```
#include <stdio.h>

float celsius(float fahr);

/* print Fahrenheit-Celsius table
    for fahr = 0, 20, . . ., 300; floating-point version      */
main()
{
    float fahr;
    int lower, upper, step;

    lower = 0;           /* lower limit of temperature table */
    upper = 300;         /* upper limit                      */
    step  = 20;          /* step size                        */

    fahr = lower;
    while (fahr <= upper) {
        printf("%3.0f %6.1f\n", fahr, celsius(fahr));
        fahr = fahr + step;
    }
}

/* celsius: convert fahr into celsius                         */
float celsius(float fahr)
{
    return (5.0/9.0) * (fahr-32.0);
}
```

We use a function to convert Fahrenheit into Celsius. The name of the function is celsius, it receives a floating-point value, and it returns another floating-point value. The function returns the value of the expression via the return statement. Sometimes the expression is a simple variable, as in the function power (page 26 K&R). Sometimes we use a more involved expression, as in the function celsius, because all the work can be done in the return statement. We declared

```
float celsius(float fahr);
```

because the function expects a floating-point value and returns another floating-point value after the conversion.

Exercise 1-16: (page 30 K&R)

Revise the main routine of the longest-line program so it will correctly print the
length of arbitrarily long input lines, and as much as possible of the text.

```
#include <stdio.h>
#define   MAXLINE 1000          /* maximum input line size    */

int getline(char line[], int maxline);
void copy(char to[], char from[]);

/* print longest input line                                   */
main()
{
    int len;                 /* current line length        */
    int max;                 /* maximum length seen so far */
    char line[MAXLINE];      /* current input line         */
    char longest[MAXLINE];   /* longest line saved here    */

    max = 0;
    while ((len = getline(line, MAXLINE)) > 0) {
        printf("%d, %s", len, line);
        if (len > max) {
            max = len;
            copy(longest, line);
        }
    }
    if (max > 0)              /* there was a line           */
        printf("%s", longest);
    return 0;
}

/* getline: read a line into s, return length               */
int getline(char s[], int lim)
{
    int c, i, j;

    j = 0;
    for (i = 0; (c = getchar()) !=EOF && c != '\n'; ++i)
        if (i < lim-2) {
            s[j] = c;         /* line still in boundaries */
            ++j;
        }
```

```
    if (c == '\n') {
        s[j] = c;
        ++j;
        ++i;
    }
    s[j] = '\0';
    return i;
}

/* copy: copy 'from' into 'to'; assume to is big enough  */
void copy (char to[], char from[])
{
    int i;

    i = 0;
    while ((to[i] = from[i]) != '\0')
        ++i;
}
```

The only revision in the main routine is

```
printf("%d, %s", len, line);
```

This prints the length of the input line (len) and as many characters as it is possible to save in the array line.

The function getline has a few modifications.

```
for (i = 0; (c = getchar()) != EOF && c != '\n'; ++i)
```

The test for the limit of characters is not performed in the for loop anymore. This limit is not a condition for termination because getline now returns the length of arbitrarily long input lines and saves as much text as possible. The statement

```
if (i < lim-2)
```

determines if there is room in the array (still within boundaries). The original test in the for loop was

```
i < lim-1
```

It was changed because the last index of the array s is

```
lim-1
```

since s has lim elements and we already read the input character. So

```
i < lim-2
```

leaves room for a possible newline character

```
s[lim-2] = '\n'
```

and an end of string marker

```
s[lim-1] = '\0'
```

The length of the string is returned in `i`; `j` keeps track of the number of characters copied to the string `s`.

Exercise 1-17: (page 31 K&R)

Write a program to print all input lines that are longer than 80 characters.

```
#include <stdio.h>
#define  MAXLINE  1000     /* maximum input line size    */
#define  LONGLINE  80

int getline(char line[], int maxline);

/* print lines longer than LONGLINE                      */
main()
{
    int len;                        /* current line length */
    char line[MAXLINE];             /* current input line  */

    while ((len = getline(line, MAXLINE)) > 0)
        if (len > LONGLINE)
            printf("%s", line);
    return 0;
}
```

The program invokes getline to read an input line. getline returns the length of the line and as much text as possible. If the length is greater than 80 characters (LONGLINE), then the program prints the input line. Otherwise, no action is taken. The loop repeats until getline returns length zero.

The function getline is the same as in Exercise 1-16.

Exercise 1-18: (page 31 K&R)

Write a program to remove trailing blanks and tabs from each line of input, and to delete entirely blank lines.

```
#include   <stdio.h>
#define   MAXLINE   1000       /* maximum input line size    */

int getline(char line[], int maxline);
int remove(char s[]);

/* remove trailing blanks and tabs, and delete blank lines */
main()
{
     char line[MAXLINE];       /* current input line         */

     while (getline(line, MAXLINE) > 0)
         if (remove(line) > 0)
             printf("%s", line);
     return 0;
}


/* remove trailing blanks and tabs from character string s */
int remove (char s[])
{
     int i;

     i = 0;
     while (s[i] != '\n')   /* find newline character      */
         ++i;
     --i;                        /* back off from '\n'          */
     while (i >= 0 && (s[i] == ' ' || s[i] == '\t'))
         --i;
     if (i >= 0) {               /* is it a nonblank line?      */
         ++i;
         s[i] = '\n';        /* put newline character back */
         ++i;
         s[i] = '\0';        /* terminate the string        */
     }
     return i;
}
```

The remove function removes trailing blanks and tabs from the character string line and returns its new length. If this length is greater than 0, line has characters other than blanks and tabs, and the program prints the line. Otherwise, line is entirely made up of blanks and tabs, and thus ignored. This ensures that entirely blank lines are not printed.

The `remove` function finds the newline character and backs off one position. The function then steps backward over blanks and tabs until it finds some other character or no more characters are available ($i < 0$). If $i >= 0$, then there is at least one character. `remove` puts back the newline and the end of string marker, then returns i.

The function `getline` is the same as in Exercise 1-16.

Exercise 1-19: (page 31 K&R)

Write a function `reverse(s)` that reverses the character string `s`. Use it to write a program that reverses its input a line at a time.

```
#include  <stdio.h>
#define   MAXLINE   1000      /* maximum input line size   */

int getline(char line[], int maxline);
void reverse(char s[]);

/* reverse input lines, a line at a time                   */
main()
{
      char line[MAXLINE];         /* current input line     */

      while (getline(line, MAXLINE) > 0) {
            reverse(line);
            printf("%s", line);
      }
}

/* reverse: reverse string s                               */
void reverse(char s[])
{
      int i, j;
      char temp;

      i = 0;
      while (s[i] != '\0')        /* find the end of string s   */
            ++i;
      --i;                        /* back off from '\0'         */
      if (s[i] == '\n')
            --i;                  /* leave newline in place     */
      j = 0;                      /* beginning of new string s  */
      while (j < i) {
            temp = s[j];
            s[j] = s[i];          /* swap the characters        */
            s[i] = temp;
            --i;
            ++j;
      }
}
```

The `reverse` function first finds the end of string `s`. It then backs off one position from `'\0'`, so that the first character will not become an end of string marker. If a '\n' exists, it backs off one more position, since like the '\0', it must remain at the end of the line.

j is the index of the first character of the string, and i is the index of the last character of the string. While swapping characters, j is incremented (moves toward the end of the string), and i is decremented (moves toward the beginning of the string). The process continues while j is less than i.

The main program reads a line of input at a time, reverses it, and prints the reversed line.

The function getline is the same as in Exercise 1-16.

Exercise 1-20: (page 34 K&R)

Write a program detab that replaces tabs in the input with the proper number
of blanks to space to the next tab stop. Assume a fixed set of tab stops, say
every *n* columns.   Should *n* be a variable or a symbolic parameter?

```c
#include <stdio.h>

#define   TABINC   8      /* tab increment size                    */

/* replace tabs with the proper number of blanks                   */
main()
{
    int c, nb, pos;

    nb = 0;                  /* number of blanks necessary      */
    pos = 1;                 /* position of character in line   */
    while ((c = getchar()) != EOF) {
        if (c == '\t') {           /* tab character            */
            nb = TABINC - (pos - 1) % TABINC;
            while (nb > 0) {
                putchar(' ');
                ++pos;
                --nb;
            }
        } else if (c == '\n' {  /* newline character        */
            putchar(c);
            pos = 1;
        } else {                   /* all other characters     */
            putchar(c);
            ++pos;
        }
    }
}
```

The tab stops are at every TABINC position.   In this program TABINC is defined
to be 8.   The variable pos is the position within a line of text where the program
currently is.

   If the character is a tab, the program calculates the number of blanks nb
necessary to reach the next tab stop. The statement

```c
nb = TABINC - (pos - 1) % TABINC
```

determines this value.   If the character is a newline, then it is printed out and
pos is reinitialized to the beginning of the line (pos = 1).   Any other character
is printed and pos is incremented (++pos).

TABINC is a symbolic constant.   Later on, in Chapter 5, you will learn how to pass arguments to the main program and you may want to allow the user to set the number of columns between tab stops.   Then you may want to change TABINC into a variable.

The program detab is extended in Exercises 5-11 and 5-12.

Exercise 1-21: (page 34 K&R)

Write the program `entab` that replaces strings of blanks by the minimum number
of tabs and blanks to achieve the same spacing.   Use the same tab stops as for
`detab`.   When either a tab or a single blank would suffice to reach a tab stop,
which should be given preference?

```
#include   <stdio.h>

#define   TABINC   8                          /* tab increment size    */

/* replace strings of blanks with tabs and blanks                      */
main()
{
    int c, nb, nt, pos;

    nb = 0;                               /* # of blanks necessary */
    nt = 0;                               /* # of tabs necessary   */
    for (pos = 1; (c = getchar()) != EOF; ++pos)
        if (c == ' ') {
            if (pos % TABINC != 0)
                ++nb;                     /* increment # of blanks */
            else {
                nb = 0;                   /* reset # of blanks     */
                ++nt;                     /* one more tab          */
            }
        } else {
            for ( ; nt > 0; --nt)
                putchar('\t');            /* output tab(s)         */
            if (c == '\t')                /* forget the blank(s)   */
                nb = 0;
            else                          /* output blank(s)       */
                for ( ; nb > 0; --nb)
                    putchar(' ');
            putchar(c);
            if (c == '\n')
                pos = 0;
            else if (c == '\t')
                pos = pos + (TABINC - (pos-1) % TABINC) - 1;
        }
}
```

The integer variables `nb` and `nt` are the minimum number of blanks and tabs
necessary to replace a string of blanks.   The variable `pos` is the position within
a line of text where the program currently is.

The idea is to find all blanks.   A string of blanks is replaced by a tab every
time `pos` reaches a multiple of `TABINC`.

When the program finds a nonblank, then it prints the tabs and blanks accumulated followed by the nonblank character. The program resets nb and nt to zero, and resets pos to the beginning of the line if the current character is a newline.

If the nonblank character is a tab, then the program prints only the accumulated tabs followed by the current tab character.

When a single blank suffices to reach a tab stop, it is easier to replace it with a tab because we avoid special cases.

The program entab is extended in Exercises 5-11 and 5-12.

Exercise 1-22: (page 34 K&R)

Write a program to "fold" long input lines into two or more shorter lines after
the last nonblank character that occurs before the *n*-th column of input.   Make
sure your program does something intelligent with very long lines, and if there
are no blanks or tabs before the specified column.

```
#include <stdio.h>

#define    MAXCOL    10         /* maximum column of input    */
#define    TABINC    8          /* tab increment size         */

char line[MAXCOL];              /* input line                 */

int exptab(int pos);
int findblnk(int pos);
int newpos(int pos);
void printl(int pos);

/* fold long input lines into two or more shorter lines       */
main()
{
     int c, pos;

     pos = 0;                   /* position in the line        */
     while ((c = getchar()) != EOF) {
          line[pos] = c;        /* store current character     */
          if (c == '\t')        /* expand tab character        */
               pos = exptab(pos);
          else if (c == '\n') {
               printl(pos);     /* print current input line    */
               pos = 0;
          } else if (++pos >= MAXCOL) {
               pos = findblnk(pos);
               printl(pos);
               pos = newpos(pos);
          }
     }
}

/* printl: print line until pos column                        */
void printl(int pos)
{
     int i;
```

```
        for (i = 0; i < pos; ++i)
            putchar(line[i]);
        if (pos > 0)              /* any chars printed ?      */
            putchar('\n');
}

/* exptab: expand tab into blanks                              */
int exptab(int pos)
{
        line[pos] = ' ';          /* tab is at least one blank */
        for (++pos; pos < MAXCOL && pos % TABINC != 0; ++pos)
            line[pos] = ' ';
        if (pos < MAXCOL)         /* room left in current line */
            return pos;
        else {                    /* current line is full      */
            print1(pos);
            return 0;             /* reset current position    */
        }
}

/* findblnk: find blank's position                             */
int findblnk(int pos)
{
        while (pos > 0 && line[pos] != ' ')
            --pos;
        if (pos == 0)             /* no blanks in the line ?   */
            return MAXCOL;
        else                      /* at least one blank        */
            return pos+1;         /* position after the blank  */
}

/* newpos: rearrange line with new position                    */
int newpos(int pos)
{
        int i, j;

        if (pos <= 0 || pos >= MAXCOL)
            return 0;             /* nothing to rearrange      */
        else {
            i = 0;
            for (j = pos; j < MAXCOL; ++j) {
                line[i] = line[j];
                ++i;
            }
            return i;             /* new position in line      */
        }
}
```

MAXCOL is a symbolic constant. It indicates the *n*-th column of input. The integer variable pos points to the position within a line of text where the program currently is. The program folds input lines before the *n*-th column of input.

The program expands tab characters, prints the current input when it finds a newline, and folds the input line when pos reaches MAXCOL.

The function findblnk searches for a blank starting at the index pos. It returns the position after a blank or MAXCOL if a blank does not exist.

printl prints the characters between position zero and pos-1.

newpos rearranges a line, that is, it copies characters, starting at pos, to the beginning of the line, then returns the new value of pos.

Exercise 1-23: (page 34 K&R)

Write a program to remove all comments from a C program.   Don't forget to handle quoted strings and character constants properly.   C comments do not nest.

```
#include <stdio.h>

void rcomment(int c);
void in_comment(void);
void echo_quote(int c);

/* remove all comments from a valid C program              */
main()
{
     int c, d;

     while ((c = getchar()) != EOF)
         rcomment(c);
     return 0;
}

/* rcomment: read each character, remove the comments      */
void rcomment(int c)
{
     int d;

     if (c == '/')
         if ((d = getchar()) == '*')
             in_comment();                 /*beginning comment*/
         else if (d == '/') {
             putchar(c);                   /*another slash    */
             rcomment(d);
         } else {
             putchar(c);                   /* not a comment   */
             putchar(d);
         }
     else if (c == '\'' || c == '"')
         echo_quote(c);                    /* quote begins    */
     else
         putchar(c);                       /* not a comment   */
}
```

```
/* in_comment: inside of a valid comment                       */
void in_comment(void)
{
    int c, d;

    c = getchar();                          /* prev character   */
    d = getchar();                          /* curr character   */
    while (c != '*' || d != '/') {          /* search for end   */
        c = d;
        d = getchar();
    }
}


/* echo_quote: echo characters within quotes                   */
void echo_quote(int c)
{
    int d;

    putchar(c);
    while ((d = getchar()) != c) {    /* search for end     */
        putchar(d);
        if (d == '\\')
            putchar(getchar());       /* ignore escape seq*/
    }
    putchar(d);
}
```

The program assumes that the input is a valid C program. rcomment searches for the beginning of a comment (/*) and when it finds it calls in_comment. This function searches for the end of the comment. The procedure therefore ensures that a comment will be ignored.

rcomment also searches for single and double quotes and if it finds them calls echo_quote. The argument to echo_quote indicates whether it is a single or double quote. echo_quote ensures that anything within a quote is echoed and not mistaken for a comment. echo_quote does not consider a quote following a backslash as the terminating quote (see the discussion on escape sequences on page 19 K&R and in Exercise 1-2). Any other character is printed as is.

The program terminates when getchar returns an end of file.

Exercise 1-24: (page 34 K&R)

Write a program to check a C program for rudimentary syntax errors like unbalanced parentheses, brackets, and braces. Don't forget about quotes, both
single and double, escape sequences, and comments. (This program is hard if
you do it in full generality.)

```c
#include <stdio.h>

int brace, brack, paren;

void in_quote(int c);
void in_comment(void);
void search(int c);

/* rudimentary syntax checker for C programs              */
main()
{
    int c;
    extern int brace, brack, paren;

    while ((c = getchar()) != EOF) {
        if (c == '/') {
            if ((c = getchar()) == '*')
                in_comment();        /* inside comment   */
            else
                search(c);
        } else if (c == '\'' || c == '"')
            in_quote(c);             /* inside quote     */
        else
            search(c);

        if (brace < 0) {             /* output errors    */
            printf("Unbalanced braces\n");
            brace = 0;
        } else if (brack < 0) {
            printf("Unbalanced brackets\n");
            brack = 0;
        } else if (paren < 0) {
            printf("Unbalanced parentheses\n");
            paren = 0;
        }
    }
}
```

```
    if (brace > 0)                              /* output errors   */
        printf("Unbalanced braces\n");
    if (brack > 0)
        printf("Unbalanced brackets\n");
    if (paren > 0)
        printf("Unbalanced parentheses\n");
}

/* search: search for rudimentary syntax errors                   */
void search(int c)
{
    extern int brace, brack, paren;

    if (c == '{')
        ++brace;
    else if (c == '}')
        --brace;
    else if (c == '[')
        ++brack;
    else if (c == ']')
        --brack;
    else if (c == '(')
        ++paren;
    else if (c == ')')
        --paren;
}

/* in_comment: inside of a valid comment                          */
void in_comment(void)
{
    int c, d;

    c = getchar();                      /* prev character   */
    d = getchar();                      /* curr character   */
    while (c != '*' || d != '/') {      /* search for end   */
        c = d;
        d = getchar();
    }
}
```

```
/* in_quote: inside quote                              */
void in_quote(int c)
{
    int d;

    while ((d = getchar()) != c)         /* search end quote */
        if (d == '\\')
            getchar();                   /* ignore escape seq */
}
```

This solution is not done in full generality.

The program checks for three syntax errors: unbalanced parentheses, brackets, and braces. Everything else is assumed to be valid.

The function `search` increments the variable `brace` when the character is a left brace (`{`) and decrements it when the character is a right brace (`}`). The variables `brack` and `paren` are handled similarly.

During the search, it is legal for `brace`, `brack`, or `paren` to be positive or zero. It is an error if `brace`, `brack`, or `paren` ever becomes negative; the program prints an appropriate message. `[[[` (`brack` equals 3) is legal for the moment because 3 balancing right brackets might be found later in the search. `]]]` (`brack` equals -3) is illegal because there were no previous left brackets to balance these 3 right brackets; if there were 3 left brackets to balance them, then `brack` should equal 0. The statements

```
if (brace < 0) {
    printf("Unbalanced braces\n");
    brace = 0;
} else if (brack < 0) {
    printf("Unbalanced brackets\n");
    brack = 0;
} else if (paren < 0) {
    printf("Unbalanced parentheses\n");
    paren = 0;
}
```

are necessary because without them `)(` or `]][[` or `}}{{` would be considered balanced.

The main routine searches for comments, single and double quotes, and skips the characters within them. The braces, brackets, and parentheses inside comments and quotes need not be balanced.

The program makes a final check upon `EOF` to determine if there are any open braces, brackets, or parentheses. If so, the program prints an appropriate message.

CHAPTER 2   Types, Operators, and Expressions

Exercise 2-1: (page 36 K&R)

Write a program to determine the ranges of char, short, int, and long
variables, both signed and unsigned, by printing appropriate values from
standard headers and by direct computation. Harder if you compute them:
determine the ranges of the various floating-point types.

```
#include    <stdio.h>
#include    <limits.h>

/* determine ranges of types                                 */
main()
{
    /* signed types                                          */
    printf("signed char min  = %d\n", SCHAR_MIN);
    printf("signed char max  = %d\n", SCHAR_MAX);
    printf("signed short min = %d\n", SHRT_MIN);
    printf("signed short max = %d\n", SHRT_MAX);
    printf("signed int min   = %d\n", INT_MIN);
    printf("signed int max   = %d\n", INT_MAX);
    printf("signed long min  = %ld\n", LONG_MIN);
    printf("signed long max  = %ld\n", LONG_MAX);
    /* unsigned types                                        */
    printf("unsigned char max  = %u\n", UCHAR_MAX);
    printf("unsigned short max = %u\n", USHRT_MAX);
    printf("unsigned int max   = %u\n", UINT_MAX);
    printf("unsigned long max  = %lu\n", ULONG_MAX);
}
```

    The ANSI standard for C specifies that ranges be defined in <limits.h>.
The ranges may vary from machine to machine because the sizes for short,
int, and long vary for different hardware.

```
#include  <stdio.h>

/* determine ranges of types                                   */
main()
{
    /* signed types                                            */
    printf("signed char min  = %d\n",
                        -(char)((unsigned char) ~0 >> 1));
    printf("signed char max  = %d\n",
                        (char)((unsigned char) ~0 >> 1));
    printf("signed short min = %d\n",
                        -(short)((unsigned short) ~0 >> 1));
    printf("signed short max = %d\n",
                        (short)((unsigned short) ~0 >> 1));
    printf("signed int min   = %d\n",
                        -(int)((unsigned int) ~0 >> 1));
    printf("signed int max   = %d\n",
                        (int)((unsigned int) ~0 >> 1));
    printf("signed long min  = %ld\n",
                        -(long)((unsigned long) ~0 >> 1));
    printf("signed long max  = %ld\n",
                        (long)((unsigned long) ~0 >> 1));
    /* unsigned types                                          */
    printf("unsigned char max  = %u\n",
                        (unsigned char) ~0);
    printf("unsigned short max = %u\n",
                        (unsigned short) ~0);
    printf("unsigned int max   = %u\n",
                        (unsigned int) ~0);
    printf("unsigned long max  = %lu\n",
                        (unsigned long) ~0);
}
```

    Another possible solution uses bitwise operators (page 48 K&R). For
example, the expression

```
(char)((unsigned char) ~0 >> 1)
```

takes a zero and converts each bit to one

```
~0
```

then converts the resulting quantity to an `unsigned char`

```
(unsigned char) ~0
```

and shifts the `unsigned char` one position to the right to clear the sign bit

```
(unsigned char) ~0 >> 1
```

and finally converts the quantity to `char`

```
(char)((unsigned char) ~0 >> 1)
```

That is the maximum value for a `signed` character.

Exercise 2-2: (page 42 K&R)

Write a loop equivalent to the `for` loop above without using `&&` or `!!`.

Original:

```
for (i=0; i<lim-1 && (c=getchar()) != '\n' && c != EOF; ++i)
```

Equivalent:

```
enum loop { NO, YES };
enum loop okloop = YES;

i = 0;
while (okloop == YES)
    if (i >= lim-1)              /* outside of valid range ?   */
        okloop = NO;
    else if ((c = getchar()) == '\n')
        okloop = NO;
    else if (c == EOF)           /* end of file ?              */
        okloop = NO;
    else {
        s[i] = c;
        ++i;
    }
```

Without `&&` or `!!` we have to break the original `for` loop into a sequence of `if` statements. We then change the tests. For example, in the original `for` loop

```
    i < lim-1
```

indicates that `i` still is within boundaries. In the equivalent statement

```
    i >= lim-1
```

indicates that `i` is out of boundaries and the loop should terminate.

okloop is an enumeration. As soon as one of the conditions is met okloop is set to NO and the loop terminates.

Exercise 2-3: (page 46 K&R)

Write the function htoi(s), which converts a string of hexadecimal digits (including an optional 0x or 0X) into its equivalent integer value.   The allowable digits are 0 through 9, a through f, and A through F.

```
#define    YES        1
#define    NO         0

/* htoi: convert hexadecimal string s to integer                    */
int htoi(char s[])
{
    int hexdigit, i, inhex, n;

    i = 0;
    if (s[i] == '0') {            /* skip optional 0x or 0X          */
        ++i;
        if (s[i] == 'x' || s[i] == 'X')
            ++i;
    }
    n = 0;                        /* integer value to be returned    */
    inhex = YES;                  /* assume valid hexadecimal digit  */
    for ( ; inhex == YES; ++i) {
        if (s[i] >= '0' && s[i] <= '9')
            hexdigit = s[i] - '0';
        else if (s[i] >= 'a' && s[i] <= 'f')
            hexdigit = s[i] - 'a' + 10;
        else if (s[i] >= 'A' && s[i] <= 'F')
            hexdigit = s[i] - 'A' + 10;
        else
            inhex = NO;    /* not a valid hexadecimal digit   */
        if (inhex == YES)
            n = 16 * n + hexdigit;
    }
    return n;
}
```

The statement

```
for ( ; inhex == YES; ++i)
```

controls the function.   The integer i is the index for the array s.   While s[i] is a valid hexadecimal digit, inhex remains YES and the loop continues.   The variable hexdigit takes a numerical value of 0 through 15.

The statement

```
if (inhex == YES)
```

guarantees that a valid hexadecimal digit was at `s[i]` and its value is in `hexdigit`. When the loop terminates, `htoi` returns the value of the variable `n`.

This function is similar to `atoi` (page 43 K&R).

Exercise 2-4: (page 48 K&R)

Write an alternate version of `squeeze(s1,s2)` that deletes each character in
`s1` that matches any character in the *string* `s2`.

```
/* squeeze: delete each char in s1 which is in s2                    */
void squeeze(char s1[], char s2[])
{
    int i, j, k;

    for (i = k = 0; s1[i] != '\0'; i++) {
        for (j = 0; s2[j] != '\0' && s2[j] != s1[i]; j++)
            ;
        if (s2[j] == '\0')                /* end of string - no match */
            s1[k++] = s1[i];
    }
    s1[k] = '\0';
}
```

The first statement,

```
for (i = k = 0; s1[i] != '\0'; i++)
```

initializes `i` and `k`, the indexes of `s1` and the resulting string (also `s1`), respectively. Each character in `s1` that matches any character in `s2` is deleted. The
loop continues until the end of the string `s1`.
     The second `for` statement checks each character in `s2` against the `s1[i]`
character. This loop terminates when `s2` runs out of characters or there is a
match. In the event that there is no match, `s1[i]` is copied to the resulting
string. If there is a match, the statement

```
if (s2[j] == '\0')
```

fails, and `s1[i]` is not copied to the resulting string (it is squeezed out).

Exercise 2-5: (page 48 K&R)

Write the function any(s1,s2), which returns the first location in the string
s1 where any character from the string s2 occurs, or -1 if s1 contains no
characters from s2. (The standard library function strpbrk does the same
job but returns a pointer to the location.)

```
/* any: return first location in s1 where any char from s2 occurs*/
int any(char s1[], char s2[])
{
     int i, j;

     for (i = 0; s1[i] != '\0'; i++)
          for (j = 0; s2[j] != '\0'; j++)
               if (s1[i] == s2[j])          /* match found?          */
                    return i;                /* location first match  */
     return -1;                              /* otherwise, no match   */
}
```

The statement

```
for (i = 0; s1[i] != '\0'; i++)
```

controls the loop. When the loop terminates normally (s1 runs out of characters),
any returns -1 to indicate that no character of s2 was found in s1.
     The second for statement,

```
for (j = 0; s2[j] != '\0'; j++)
```

is executed for each value of i. It compares each character of s2 with s1[i].
When a character in s2 matches s1[i] the function returns i —the first location
in the string s1 where any character from the string s2 occurs.

Exercise 2-6: (page 49 K&R)

Write a function `setbits(x,p,n,y)` that returns x with the n bits that begin at position p set to the rightmost n bits of y, leaving the other bits unchanged.

```
/* setbits: set n bits of x at position p with bits of y     */
unsigned setbits(unsigned x, int p, int n, unsigned y)
{
     return x & ~(~(~0 << n)  << (p+1-n)) |
            (y &  ~(~0 << n)) << (p+1-n);
}
```

To set n bits of x to the rightmost n bits of y

```
      xxx...xnnnx...xxx   x
      yyy...........ynnn  y
```

we need to clear the n bits in x, clear all bits in y except the rightmost n bits and then shift them to position p, and OR the quantities together.

```
      xxx...x000x...xxx   x
      000...0nnn0...000   y
      -----------------------
      xxx...xnnnx...xxx   x
```

To clear the n bits in x we AND them with n bits of zeros starting at position p and ones everywhere else.

```
~0 << n
```

shifts all ones n positions to the left, leaving n zeros at the rightmost positions.

```
~(~0 << n)
```

places all ones at the rightmost n positions, zeros everywhere else.

```
~(~0 << n) << (p+1-n)
```

shifts these n 1-bits to position p and

```
~(~(~0 << n) << (p+1-n))
```

sets n bits to zeros starting at position p, leaving ones everywhere else.

```
x & ~(~(~0 << n) << (p+1-n))
```

we AND this value with x to clear the n bits of x at position p.

    To clear all bits in y except the rightmost n bits we AND them with n bits of ones and zeros everywhere else.

```
~(~0 << n)
```

places all ones at the rightmost n positions, zeros everywhere else.

```
y & ~(~0 << n)
```

selects the rightmost n bits of y.   And

```
(y & ~(~0 << n)) << (p+1-n)
```

places these n bits starting at position p.

```
  x & ~(~(~0 << n)  << (p+1-n)) |
 (y &  ~ (~0 << n)) << (p+1-n)
```

we OR the two values to set the n bits of x starting at position p to the rightmost n bits of y, leaving the other bits unchanged.

Exercise 2-7: (page 49 K&R)

Write a function `invert(x,p,n)` that returns x with the n bits that begin at position p inverted (i.e., 1 changed into 0 and vice versa), leaving the others unchanged.

```
/* invert: inverts the n bits of x that begin at position p */
unsigned invert(unsigned x, int p, int n)
{
    return x ^ (~(~0 << n) << (p+1-n));
}
```

`(~0 << n)`

shifts all ones n positions to the left, leaving n zeros at the rightmost positions.

`~(~0 << n)`

places all ones at the rightmost positions, zeros everywhere else.

`(~(~0 << n) << (p+1-n))`

shifts these n 1-bits to position p.

`x ^ (~(~0 << n) << (p+1-n))`

The bitwise exclusive OR operator (^) produces a 1 when two bits are different, otherwise it produces a 0. Since the objective is to invert the n bits starting at position p, it suffices to exclusive OR them with all ones starting at p for n bits (with zeros everywhere else). If the original bit is 0, exclusive OR with a 1 produces a 1—it is inverted. If the original bit is a 1, exclusive OR with a 1 produces a 0—it is inverted.

The positions outside of the n-bit field are exclusive OR'ed with zeros: 0 ^ 0 (bits are the same) produces a 0—nothing changed; 1 ^ 0 (bits are different) produces a 1—nothing changed. Only the n bits are inverted.

Exercise 2-8: (page 49 K&R)

Write a function rightrot(x,n) that returns the value of the integer x rotated
to the right by n bit positions.

```
/* rightrot: rotate x to the right by n positions          */
unsigned rightrot(unsigned x, int n)
{
    int wordlength(void);
    int rbit;                       /* rightmost bit              */

    while (n-- > 0) {
        rbit = (x & 1) << (wordlength() - 1);
        x = x >> 1;                 /* shift x 1 position right    */
        x = x | rbit;               /* complete one rotation       */
    }
    return x;
}
```

The variable rbit takes the rightmost bit of x and shifts it to the leftmost
position (wordlength() - 1).

Next, we shift x one position to the right and OR it with rbit to complete
one rotation. rightrot rotates x n times.

wordlength() is a function that computes the word length on the host
machine.

```
/* wordlength: computes word length of the machine          */
int wordlength(void)
{
    int i;
    unsigned v = (unsigned) ~0;

    for (i = 1; (v = v >> 1) > 0; i++)
        ;
    return i;
}
```

This is a different solution to the same exercise:

```
/* rightrot: rotate x to the right by n positions                    */
unsigned rightrot(unsigned x, int n)
{
     int wordlength(void);
     unsigned rbits;

     if ((n = n % wordlength()) > 0) {
         rbits = ~(~0 << n) & x;   /* n rightmost bits of x         */
                                   /* n rightmost bits to left      */
         rbits = rbits << (wordlength() - n);
         x = x >> n;               /* x shifted n positions right   */
         x = x | rbits;            /* rotation completed            */
     }
     return x;
}
```

If the number of positions (n) to rotate to the right is the same as the number of bits in an unsigned integer, nothing changes because x is the same as before the rotation.   If n is less, then it is necessary to rotate n positions.   If n exceeds the number of bits in an unsigned integer, then the number of rotations is the remainder (modulus operator) of n divided by the length of the word.   As a result, no looping is necessary.

> ~0 << n   all ones are shifted n positions to the left
>   leaving n zeros in the rightmost positions.
> ~(~0 << n)   all ones are in the n rightmost positions.

When we AND this value with x, the n rightmost bits of x are assigned to rbits. Then we move rbits to the leftmost position.   We shift x n positions to the right.   The new value of x is OR'ed with rbits to complete the rotation of the unsigned x, n positions to the right.

Exercise 2-9: (page 51 K&R)

In a two's complement number system, x &= (x-1) deletes the rightmost 1-bit in x. Explain why. Use this observation to write a faster version of bit-count.

```
/* bitcount: count 1 bits in x - faster version          */
int bitcount(unsigned x)
{
    int b;

    for (b = 0; x != 0; x &= x-1)
        ++b;
    return b;
}
```

Take a value for x-1, for example, the binary number 1010, which is 10 in decimal. (x-1) + 1 produces x:

binary		decimal
1010	x – 1	10
+ 1		+ 1
1011	x	11

We take (x-1) and add 1 to it to produce x. The rightmost 0-bit of x-1 changes to 1 in the result x. Therefore, the rightmost 1-bit of x has a corresponding 0-bit in x-1. This is why x & (x-1), in a two's complement number system, will delete the rightmost 1-bit in x.

Consider an unsigned quantity of four bits. To count all 1-bits in this quantity, the original bitcount performs four shifts to check the rightmost bit. An alternative is to use the knowledge that x & (x-1) turns off the rightmost 1-bit of x. For example, if x equals 9,

    1 0 0 1 value 9 in binary (x)
    1 0 0 0 value 8 (x-1)
    1 0 0 0 x & (x-1)

and the rightmost 1-bit in x has been deleted. The resulting value is 1000 in binary, 8 in decimal. Repeating the process,

    1 0 0 0 value 8 in binary (x)
    0 1 1 1 value 7 (x-1)
    0 0 0 0 x & (x-1)

and the rightmost 1-bit in x has been deleted.   The resulting value is 0000 in binary, 0 in decimal.   There are no more 1-bits in x and the process terminates.

The worst case is when all bits of x are ones—the number of AND's is the same as the number of shifts in `bitcount`.   Overall, this a faster version.

Exercise 2-10: (page 52 K&R)

Rewrite the function `lower`, which converts upper case letters to lower case, with a conditional expression instead of `if-else`.

```
/* lower: convert c to lower case (ASCII only)              */
int lower(int c)
{
     return c >= 'A' && c <= 'Z' ? c + 'a' - 'A' : c;
}
```

When the condition

```
c >= 'A' && c <= 'Z'
```

is true, c is an upper case letter (ASCII only).   Then the expression

```
c + 'a' - 'A'
```

is evaluated and `lower` returns a lower case letter.   Otherwise, `lower` returns the character unchanged.

Exercise 3-1: (page 58 K&R)

Our binary search makes two tests inside the loop, when one would suffice (at the price of more tests outside). Write a version with only one test inside the loop and measure the difference in run-time.

```
/* binsearch: find x in v[0] <= v[1] <= . . . <= v[n-1]    */
int binsearch(int x, int v[], int n)
{
    int low, high, mid;

    low = 0;
    high = n - 1;
    mid = (low+high) / 2;
    while (low <= high && x != v[mid]) {
        if (x < v[mid])
            high = mid - 1;
        else
            low = mid + 1;
        mid = (low+high) / 2;
    }
    if (x == v[mid])
        return mid;         /* found match            */
    else
        return -1;          /* no match               */
}
```

We changed the expression in the `while` loop from

```
low <= high
```

to

```
low <= high && x != v[mid]
```

so we can use only one `if` statement inside the loop. This implies that we have to calculate `mid` before the loop starts and every time the loop is executed.

We need to have a test outside of the `while` loop to determine if the loop terminated because `x` appears in the array `v`. If `x` appears in the array, `binsearch` returns `mid`, otherwise it returns `-1`.

The difference in run-time is minimal. We did not gain much in performance and lost some in code readability. The original code on page 58 K&R reads better from top to bottom.

Exercise 3-2: (page 60 K&R)

Write a function escape(s,t) that converts characters like newline and tab
into visible escape sequences like \n and \t as it copies the string t to s. Use
a switch. Write a function for the other direction as well, converting escape
sequences into the real characters.

```
/* escape: expand newline and tab into visible sequences     */
/*         while copying the string t to s                    */
void escape(char s[], char t[])
{
    int i, j;

    for (i = j = 0; t[i] != '\0'; i++)
        switch (t[i]) {
        case '\n':                        /* newline          */
            s[j++] = '\\';
            s[j++] = 'n';
            break;
        case '\t':                        /* tab              */
            s[j++] = '\\';
            s[j++] = 't';
            break;
        default:                          /* all other chars  */
            s[j++] = t[i];
            break;
        }
    s[j] = '\0';
}
```

The statement

```
for (i = j = 0; t[i] != '\0'; i++)
```

controls the loop. The variable i is the index for the original string t, and j is
the index for the modified string s.

    There are three cases in the switch statement: '\n' for newline character,
'\t' for tab character, and default. If the character t[i] does not match
one of the two cases, escape executes the case labeled default: copy
t[i] to string s.

The function unescape is similar:

```
/* unescape: convert escape sequences into real characters  */
/*            while copying the string t to s               */
void unescape(char s[], char t[])
{
    int i, j;

    for (i = j = 0; t[i] != '\0'; i++)
        if (t[i] != '\\')
            s[j++] = t[i];
        else                                /* it is a backslash*/
            switch(t[++i]) {
            case 'n':                       /* real newline      */
                s[j++] = '\n';
                break;
            case 't':                       /* real tab          */
                s[j++] = '\t';
                break;
            default:                        /* all other chars   */
                s[j++] = '\\';
                s[j++] = t[i];
                break;
            }
    s[j] = '\0';
}
```

If the character in t[i] is a backslash, then we use a switch statement to convert \n into newline and \t into tab. The default handles a backslash followed by anything else—copies a backslash and t[i] to string s.

switch statements can be nested. Here is another solution to the same problem.

```
/* unescape: convert escape sequences into real characters  */
/*            while copying the string t to s               */
void unescape(char s[], char t[])
{
    int i, j;

    for (i = j = 0; t[i] != '\0'; i++)
        switch (t[i]) {
        case '\\':                        /* backslash      */
            switch(t[++i]) {
            case 'n':                     /* real newline   */
                s[j++] = '\n';
                break;
            case 't':                     /* real tab       */
                s[j++] = '\t';
                break;
            default:                      /* all other chars */
                s[j++] = '\\';
                s[j++] = t[i];
                break;
            }
            break;
        default:                          /* not a backslash */
            s[j++] = t[i];
            break;
        }
    s[j] = '\0';
}
```

The outer `switch` statement handles the backslash character and everything else (`default`). The backslash case uses another `switch` statement as in the solution above.

Exercise 3-3: (page 63 K&R)

Write a function `expand(s1,s2)` that expands shorthand notations like `a-z` in the string `s1` into the equivalent complete list `abc...xyz` in `s2`. Allow for letters of either case and digits, and be prepared to handle cases like `a-b-c` and `a-z0-9` and `-a-z`. Arrange that a leading or trailing `-` is taken literally.

```
/* expand: expand shorthand notation in s1 into string s2   */
void expand(char s1[], char s2[])
{
    char c;
    int i, j;

    i = j = 0;
    while ((c = s1[i++]) != '\0')  /* fetch a char from s1[]*/
        if (s1[i] == '-' && s1[i+1] >= c) {
            i++;
            while (c < s1[i])     /* expand shorthand      */
                s2[j++] = c++;
        } else
            s2[j++] = c;           /* copy the character    */
    s2[j] = '\0';
}
```

   The function takes a character from `s1`, saves it in `c`, and then checks the next character. If the next character is `-` and the character after that is greater than or equal to the character in `c`, `expand` proceeds to expand the shorthand notation. Otherwise `expand` copies the character into `s2`.

   `expand` works for ASCII characters. The shorthand `a-z` expands into the equivalent list `abc...xyz`. The shorthand `!-~` expands into `!"#..ABC..XYZ..abc..xyz..}~`.

   This solution was provided by Axel Schreiner of the University of Osnabruck, West Germany.

Exercise 3-4: (page 64 K&R)

In a two's complement number representation, our version of itoa does not handle the largest negative number, that is, the value of n equal to $-(2^{\text{wordsize}-1})$. Explain why not. Modify it to print that value correctly, regardless of the machine on which it runs.

```
#define    abs(x)     ((x) < 0 ?  -(x) : (x))

/* itoa: convert n to characters in s - modified          */
void itoa(int n, char s[])
{
    int i, sign;
    void reverse(char s[]);

    sign = n;               /* record sign                 */
    i = 0;
    do {                    /* generate digits in reverse order*/
        s[i++] = abs(n % 10) + '0';   /* get next digit    */
    } while ((n /= 10) != 0);         /* delete it         */
    if (sign < 0)
        s[i++] = '-';
    s[i] = '\0';
    reverse(s);
}
```

$-(2^{\text{wordsize}-1})$

cannot be converted to a positive number as in

```
n = -n;
```

because the largest positive number in a two's complement representation is:

$(2^{\text{wordsize}-1}) - 1$

The variable sign saves the initial value of n. The macro abs finds the absolute value of n % 10. This avoids the

$-(2^{\text{wordsize}-1})$

problem because only the result of the modulus operator is made positive.

The conditional expression in the `do-while` statement has been changed from

`(n /= 10) > 0`

to

`(n /= 10) != 0`

because if n remained negative throughout the loop, the loop would be infinite.

Exercise 3-5: (page 64 K&R)

Write the function `itob(n,s,b)` that converts the integer `n` into a base `b` character representation in the string `s`. In particular, `itob(n,s,16)` formats `n` as a hexadecimal integer in `s`.

```
/*itob: convert n to characters in s - base b              */
void itob(int n, char s[], int b)
{
    int i, j, sign;
    void reverse(char s[]);

    if ((sign = n) < 0)                  /* record sign      */
        n = -n;                          /* make n positive  */
    i = 0;
    do {                 /* generate digits in reverse order */
        j = n % b;                       /* get next digit   */
        s[i++] = (j <= 9) ?  j+'0' : j+'a'-10;
    } while ((n /= b) > 0);              /* delete it         */
    if (sign < 0)
        s[i++] = '-';
    s[i] = '\0';
    reverse(s);
}
```

The contents of `n` are converted to base `b` so

`n % b`

returns a value between `0` and `b-1`, and

`n /= b`

deletes that number from `n`.   The loop continues while `n/b` is greater than zero.

Exercise 3-6: (page 64 K&R)

Write a version of itoa that accepts three arguments instead of two. The third argument is a minimum field width; the converted number must be padded with blanks on the left if necessary to make it wide enough.

```
#define    abs(x)     ((x) < 0 ?  -(x) : (x))

/* itoa: convert n to characters in s, w characters wide   */
void itoa(int n, char s[], int w)
{
    int i, sign;
    void reverse(char s[]);

    sign = n;               /* record sign                 */
    i = 0;
    do {                    /* generate digits in reverse order*/
        s[i++] = abs(n % 10) + '0';   /* get next digit   */
    } while ((n /= 10) != 0);         /* delete it         */
    if (sign < 0)
        s[i++] = '-';
    while (i < w)                     /* pad with blanks */
        s[i++] = ' ';
    s[i] = '\0';
    reverse(s);
}
```

This function is similar to itoa in Exercise 3-4. The necessary modification is

```
while (i < w)
    s[i++] = ' ';
```

The while loop pads the string s with blanks if necessary.

CHAPTER 4

Functions and Program Structure

Exercise 4-1: (page 71 K&R)

Write the function `strrindex(s,t)`, which returns the position of the *rightmost* occurrence of t in s, or -1 if there is none.

```
/* strrindex: returns rightmost index of t in s, -1 if none */
int strrindex(char s[], char t[])
{
    int i, j, k, pos;

    pos = -1;
    for (i = 0; s[i] != '\0'; i++) {
        for (j=i, k=0; t[k]!='\0' && s[j]==t[k]; j++, k++)
            ;
        if (k > 0 && t[k] == '\0')
            pos = i;
    }
    return pos;
}
```

    `strrindex` is similar to the routine `strindex` (page 69 K&R). When `strindex` finds a match it returns the position of the first element of t in s. On the other hand, `strrindex` records the position of t in s and continues searching because the function is looking for the last (rightmost) occurrence of t in s:

```
if (k > 0 && t[k] == '\0')
    pos = i;
```

    Another possible solution is:

```
#include  <string.h>

/* strrindex: returns rightmost index of t in s, -1 if none */
int strrindex(char s[], char t[])
{
    int i, j, k;

    for (i = strlen(s) - strlen(t); i >= 0; i--) {
        for (j=i, k=0; t[k]!='\0' && s[j]==t[k]; j++, k++)
            ;
        if (k > 0 && t[k] == '\0')
            return i;
    }
    return -1;
}
```

This is a more efficient solution to the same problem. It begins at the end of the string s minus the length of the string t. If there is no match strrindex steps back one position and tries again. As soon as strrindex finds t in s it returns i; i is already the rightmost position where t occurs.

Exercise 4-2: (page 73 K&R)

Extend `atof` to handle scientific notation of the form

```
123.45e-6
```

where a floating-point number may be followed by `e` or `E` and an optionally
signed exponent.

```c
#include <ctype.h>

/* atof: convert string s to double                          */
double atof(char s[])
{
    double val, power;
    int exp, i, sign;

    for (i = 0; isspace(s[i]); i++)     /* skip white space */
        ;
    sign = (s[i] == '-') ? -1 : 1;
    if (s[i] == '+' || s[i] == '-')
        i++;
    for (val = 0.0; isdigit(s[i]); i++)
        val = 10.0 * val + (s[i] - '0');
    if (s[i] == '.')
        i++;
    for (power = 1.0; isdigit(s[i]); i++) {
        val = 10.0 * val + (s[i] - '0');
        power *= 10.0;
    }
    val = sign * val / power;

    if (s[i] == 'e' || s[i] == 'E') {
        sign = (s[++i] == '-') ? -1 : 1;
        if (s[i] == '+' || s[i] == '-')
            i++;
        for (exp = 0; isdigit(s[i]); i++)
            exp = 10 * exp + (s[i] - '0');
        if (sign == 1)
            while (exp-- > 0)   /* positive exponent      */
                val *= 10;
        else
            while (exp-- > 0)   /* negative exponent      */
                val /= 10;
    }
    return val;
}
```

The first half of the routine is a duplication of atof (page 71 K&R). The function skips white spaces, records the sign, and calculates the number. At this point the original atof returns the value of the number and the modified version handles scientific notation.

The second half of the function handles the optional exponent. If an exponent does not exist then atof returns the number stored in val. If an exponent exists then the sign of the exponent is stored in the variable sign and the value of the exponent is calculated and stored in exp.

The final operation

```
if (sign == 1)
     while (exp-- > 0)
          val *= 10;
else
     while (exp-- > 0)
          val /= 10;
```

adjusts the number according to the value of the exponent. If the exponent is positive, the number is multiplied by 10 exp times. If the exponent is negative, the number is divided by 10 exp times. val then contains the final number that is returned to the calling program.

val is divided by 10 rather than multiplied by 0.1, since 0.1 is not an exact fraction in binary. In most machines, 0.1 is represented as slightly less than 0.1 and therefore 10.0 times 0.1 is rarely 1.0. Repeated division by 10 is better than repeated multiplication by 0.1, but there is still a loss of accuracy.

Exercise 4-3: (page 79 K&R)

Given the basic framework, it is straightforward to extend the calculator.   Add the modulus (%) operator and provisions for negative numbers.

```
#include    <stdio.h>
#include    <math.h>           /* for atof()                         */

#define    MAXOP      100   /* max size of operand or operator */
#define    NUMBER     '0'   /* signal that a number was found   */

int getop(char []);
void push(double);
double pop(void);

/* reverse Polish calculator                                   */
main()
{
    int type;
    double op2;
    char s[MAXOP];

    while ((type = getop(s)) != EOF) {
        switch (type) {
        case NUMBER:
            push(atof(s));
            break;
        case '+':
            push(pop() + pop());
            break;
        case '*':
            push(pop() * pop());
            break;
        case '-':
            op2 = pop();
            push(pop() - op2);
            break;
        case '/':
            op2 = pop();
            if (op2 != 0.0)
                push(pop() / op2);
            else
                printf("error: zero divisor\n");
            break;
```

```
            case '%':
                op2 = pop();
                if (op2 != 0.0)
                    push(fmod(pop(), op2));
                else
                    printf("error: zero divisor\n");
                break;
            case '\n':
                printf("\t%.8g\n", pop());
                break;
            default:
                printf("error: unknown command %s\n", s);
                break;
            }
        }
    return 0;
}
```

We made modifications to the main program and getop. The routines push and pop (page 77 K&R) remain unchanged.

The modulus operator (%) is handled like the division operator (/). The library function fmod calculates the remainder for the top two elements on the stack. op2 is the top element on the stack.

This is the modified getop:

```
#include    <stdio.h>
#include    <string.h>
#include    <ctype.h>

#define     NUMBER      '0'  /* signal that a number was found   */

int getch(void);
void ungetch(int);

/* getop: get next operator or numeric operand                  */
int getop(char s[])
{
    int c, i;

    while ((s[0] = c = getch()) == ' ' || c == '\t')
        ;
    s[1] = '\0';
    i = 0;
    if (!isdigit(c) && c != '.' && c != '-')
        return c;                   /* not a number             */
```

```
        if (c == '-')
            if (isdigit(c = getch()) || c == '.')
                s[++i] = c;             /* negative number        */
            else {
                if (c != EOF)
                    ungetch(c);
                return '-';             /* minus sign             */
            }
        if (isdigit(c))                 /* collect integer part   */
            while (isdigit(s[++i] = c = getch()))
                ;
        if (c == '.')                   /* collect fraction part  */
            while (isdigit(s[++i] = c = getch()))
                ;
        s[i] = '\0';
        if (c != EOF)
            ungetch(c);
        return NUMBER;
}
```

getop looks one character past the minus sign to determine if it is a negative number.   For example,

- 1

is a minus sign followed by a number.   But

-1.23

is a negative number.

   The extended calculator handles

```
1     -1    +
-10   3    %
```

The first expression produces zero: 1 + -1.   The second expression produces -1.

Exercise 4-4: (page 79 K&R)

Add commands to print the top element of the stack without popping, to duplicate it, and to swap the top two elements. Add a command to clear the stack.

```c
#include  <stdio.h>
#include  <math.h>        /* for atof()                              */

#define   MAXOP     100  /* max size of operand or operator */
#define   NUMBER    '0'  /* signal that a number was found  */

int getop(char []);
void push(double);
double pop(void);
void clear(void);

/* reverse Polish calculator                                          */
main()
{
    int type;
    double op1, op2;
    char s[MAXOP];

    while ((type = getop(s)) != EOF) {
        switch (type) {
        case NUMBER:
            push(atof(s));
            break;
        case '+':
            push(pop() + pop());
            break;
        case '*':
            push(pop() * pop());
            break;
        case '-':
            op2 = pop();
            push(pop() - op2);
            break;
        case '/':
            op2 = pop();
            if (op2 != 0.0)
                push(pop() / op2);
            else
                printf("error: zero divisor\n");
            break;
```

```
        case '?':        /* print top element of the stack   */
            op2 = pop();
            printf("\t%.8g\n", op2);
            push(op2);
            break;
        case 'c':        /* clear the stack                  */
            clear();
            break;
        case 'd':        /* duplicate top elem. of the stack */
            op2 = pop();
            push(op2);
            push(op2);
            break;
        case 's':        /* swap the top two elements        */
            op1 = pop();
            op2 = pop();
            push(op1);
            push(op2);
            break;
        case '\n':
            printf("\t%.8g\n", pop());
            break;
        default:
            printf("error: unknown command %s\n", s);
            break;
        }
    }
    return 0;
}
```

The newline operator pops the top element on the stack and prints it. We added a new operator, '?', that pops the top element of the stack, prints it, and pushes it back on the stack. We do not permanently pop the top element of the stack like the newline operator but we use the pop, print, push sequence to avoid letting the main program know about the stack or the stack position variables.

To duplicate the top element of the stack we pop it and push it back twice.

We swap the top two elements of the stack by popping them and by pushing them back in reverse order.

It is easy to clear the stack; set sp to zero. So we added a new function that does exactly that and we put it together with push and pop. This way only the functions that maintain the stack refer to the stack and stack position variables.

```
/* clear: clear the stack                                  */
void clear(void)
{
    sp = 0;
}
```

Exercise 4-5: (page 79 K&R)

Add access to library functions like `sin`, `exp`, and `pow`. See `<math.h>` in Appendix B, Section 4 (page 250 K&R).

```
#include    <stdio.h>
#include    <string.h>
#include    <math.h>        /* for atof()                              */

#define     MAXOP       100  /* max size of operand or operator */
#define     NUMBER      '0'  /* signal that a number was found  */
#define     NAME        'n'  /* signal that a name was found    */

int getop(char []);
void push(double);
double pop(void);
void mathfnc(char []);

/* reverse Polish calculator                                     */
main()
{
    int type;
    double op2;
    char s[MAXOP];

    while ((type = getop(s)) != EOF) {
        switch (type) {
        case NUMBER:
            push(atof(s));
            break;
        case NAME:
            mathfnc(s);
            break;
        case '+':
            push(pop() + pop());
            break;
        case '*':
            push(pop() * pop());
            break;
        case '-':
            op2 = pop();
            push(pop() - op2);
            break;
```

```
            case '/':
                op2 = pop();
                if (op2 != 0.0)
                    push(pop() / op2);
                else
                    printf("error: zero divisor\n");
                break;
            case '\n':
                printf("\t%.8g\n", pop());
                break;
            default:
                printf("error: unknown command %s\n", s);
                break;
            }
    }
    return 0;
}

/* mathfnc: check string s for supported math functions   */
void mathfnc(char s[])
{
    double op2;

    if (strcmp(s, "sin") == 0)
        push(sin(pop()));
    else if (strcmp(s, "cos") == 0)
        push(cos(pop()));
    else if (strcmp(s, "exp") == 0)
        push(exp(pop()));
    else if (strcmp(s, "pow") == 0) {
        op2 = pop();
        push(pow(pop(), op2));
    } else
        printf("error: %s not supported\n", s);
}
```

The source file for the modified getop:

```
#include    <stdio.h>
#include    <string.h>
#include    <ctype.h>

#define     NUMBER      '0'  /* signal that a number was found   */
#define     NAME        'n'  /* signal that a name was found     */

int getch(void);
void ungetch(int);
```

```
/* getop: get next operator, numeric operand, or math fnc   */
int getop(char s[])
{
    int c, i;

    while ((s[0] = c = getch()) == ' ' || c == '\t')
        ;
    s[1] = '\0';
    i = 0;
    if (islower(c)) {                  /* command or NAME       */
        while (islower(s[++i] = c = getch()))
            ;
        s[i] = '\0';
        if (c != EOF)
            ungetch(c);                /* went one char too far */
        if (strlen(s) > 1)
            return NAME;               /* >1 char; it is NAME   */
        else
            return c;                  /* it may be a command   */
    }
    if (!isdigit(c) && c != '.')
        return c;                      /* not a number          */
    if (isdigit(c))                    /* collect integer part  */
        while (isdigit(s[++i] = c = getch()))
            ;
    if (c == '.')                      /* collect fraction part */
        while (isdigit(s[++i] = c = getch()))
            ;
    s[i] = '\0';
    if (c != EOF)
        ungetch(c);
    return NUMBER;
}
```

We modified getop to be able to gather a string of lower case letters and return it with the type NAME. The main program recognizes NAME as one of the valid types and invokes mathfnc.

The routine mathfnc is new. It performs a sequence of if statements until it finds a function name that matches the string s or it reports an error. If the string s is one of the supported functions, mathfnc pops enough elements from the stack and invokes the math function. The math function returns a value and mathfnc pushes it back on the stack.

For example, sin expects an argument in radians and the sine of PI / 2 is one.

```
3.14159265 2 / sin
```

The first operation divides PI by 2 and pushes the result back on the stack. The function sin pops the top element of the stack, calculates the sine, and pushes the result back. The result is one.

```
3.141592 2 / sin 0 cos +
```

produces 2 because the sine of PI / 2 is one and the cosine of zero is one.
    Another example,

```
5 2 pow 4 2 pow +
```

raises 5 to the power 2, 4 to the power 2, and adds the two values.
    getop does not know about specific function names; it just returns strings as it finds them. This way it is straightforward to expand mathfnc to include more functions.

Exercise 4-6: (page 79 K&R)

Add commands for handling variables. (It's easy to provide twenty-six variables with single-letter names.) Add a variable for the most recently printed value.

```c
#include    <stdio.h>
#include    <math.h>        /* for atof()                         */

#define     MAXOP      100  /* max size of operand or operator */
#define     NUMBER     '0'  /* signal that a number was found   */

int getop(char []);
void push(double);
double pop(void);

/* reverse Polish calculator                                      */
main()
{
    int i, type, var = 0;
    double op2, v;
    char s[MAXOP];
    double variable[26];

    for (i = 0; i < 26; i++)
        variable[i] = 0.0;
    while ((type = getop(s)) !=EOF) {
        switch (type) {
        case NUMBER:
            push(atof(s));
            break;
        case '+':
            push(pop() + pop());
            break;
        case '*':
            push(pop() * pop());
            break;
        case '-':
            op2 = pop();
            push(pop() - op2);
            break;
        case '/':
            op2 = pop();
            if (op2 != 0.0)
                push(pop() / op2);
            else
                printf("error: zero divisor\n");
            break;
```

```
        case '=':
                pop();
                if (var >= 'A' && var <= 'Z')
                        variable[var - 'A'] = pop();
                else
                        printf("error: no variable name\n");
                break;
        case '\n':
                v = pop();
                printf("\t%.8g\n", v);
                break;
        default:
                if (type >= 'A' && type <= 'Z')
                        push(variable[type - 'A']);
                else if (type == 'v')
                        push(v);
                else
                        printf("error: unknown command %s\n", s);
                break;
        }
        var = type;
    }
    return 0;
}
```

The variables we added are upper case letters from A to Z. The letters serve as the index to the array variable. We added a lower case variable v that contains the most recently printed value.

Whenever the program finds a variable name (A-Z, or v) it pushes its value on the stack. We also have a new operator, '=', that assigns an element from the stack to the preceding variable name. For example,

```
3 A =
```

assigns the value 3 to the variable A. Then

```
2 A +
```

adds 2 to 3 (the value assigned to the variable A). At the newline operator the program prints 5 and also assigns 5 to the variable v. If the next operation is

```
v 1 +
```

it produces 6: 5 + 1.

Exercise 4-7: (page 79 K&R)

Write a routine `ungets(s)` that will push back an entire string onto the input. Should `ungets` know about `buf` and `bufp`, or should it just use `ungetch`?

```
#include  <string.h>

/* ungets: push string back onto the input              */
void ungets(char s[])
{
    int len = strlen(s);
    void ungetch(int);

    while (len > 0)
        ungetch(s[--len]);
}
```

The variable `len` contains the number of characters in the string `s` (excluding the terminating `'\0'`), which is determined by the function `strlen` (page 39 K&R).

`ungets` calls the routine `ungetch` (page 79 K&R) `len` times, each time pushing back a character from the string `s` onto the input. `ungets` pushes the string back in reverse order.

`ungets` does not need to know about `buf` and `bufp`. The routine `ungetch` handles `buf`, `bufp`, and error checking.

Exercise 4-8: (page 79 K&R)

Suppose that there will never be more than one character of pushback.   Modify
getch and ungetch accordingly.

```
#include  <stdio.h>

char buf = 0;

/* getch: get a (possibly pushed back) character              */
int getch(void)
{
     int c;

     if (buf != 0)
          c = buf;
     else
          c = getchar();
     buf = 0;
     return c;
}

/* ungetch: push character back onto the input                */
void ungetch(int c)
{
     if (buf != 0)
          printf("ungetch: too many characters\n");
     else
          buf = c;
}
```

The buffer, buf, is no longer an array because there will never be more than 1
character in the buffer at any time.
     buf is initialized to zero at load time and getch resets buf to zero every
time it gets a character.   ungetch checks for an empty buffer before it pushes
a character back.   If the buffer is not empty then ungetch produces an error
message.

Exercise 4-9: (page 79 K&R)

Our getch and ungetch do not handle a pushed-back EOF correctly. Decide what their properties ought to be if an EOF is pushed back, then implement your design.

```
#include  <stdio.h>

#define   BUFSIZE   100

int buf[BUFSIZE];          /* buffer for ungetch               */
int bufp = 0;              /* next free position in buf        */

/* getch: get a (possibly pushed back) character              */
int getch(void)
{
    return (bufp > 0) ? buf[--bufp] : getchar();
}

/* ungetch: push character back onto the input                */
void ungetch(int c)
{
    if (bufp >= BUFSIZE)
        printf("ungetch: too many characters\n");
    else
        buf[bufp++] = c;
}
```

In the routines getch and ungetch (page 79 K&R), the buffer, buf, is declared to be an array of characters:

```
char buf[BUFSIZE];
```

The C programming language does not require a char variable to be signed or unsigned (page 43 K&R). When a char is converted to an int, it might never produce a negative number. On some machines, if the leftmost bit of a char is 1, it will produce a negative number when converted to an int. On others, a char is converted to an int by adding zeros at the left end. This conversion will always produce a positive number, regardless of whether the leftmost bit was 1 or not.

In hexadecimal notation -1 is 0xFFFF (to 16 bits). When 0xFFFF is stored in a char, the actual number being stored is 0xFF. When 0xFF is converted to an `int`, it might produce 0x00FF, which is 255, or 0xFFFF, which is −1.

negative number (−1) →	character →	integer
0xFFFF	0xFF	0x00FF (255)
0xFFFF	0xFF	0xFFFF (−1)

If we are going to treat `EOF` (−1) as any other character, `buf` should be declared as an array of integers:

```
int buf[BUFSIZE];
```

No conversions will occur and `EOF` (−1) or any negative number will be handled in a portable way.

Exercise 4-10: (page 79 K&R)

An alternate organization uses `getline` to read an entire input line; this makes `getch` and `ungetch` unnecessary. Revise the calculator to use this approach.

```
#include   <stdio.h>
#include   <ctype.h>

#define   MAXLINE   100
#define   NUMBER    '0'   /* signal that a number was found   */

int getline(char line[], int limit);

int li = 0;                     /* input line index           */
char line [MAXLINE];            /* one input line             */

/* getop: get next operator or numeric operand               */
int getop(char s[])
{
    int c, i;

    if (line[li] == '\0')
        if (getline(line, MAXLINE) == 0)
            return EOF;
        else
            li = 0;
    while ((s[0] = c = line[li++]) == ' ' || c == '\t')
        ;
    s[1] = '\0';
    if (!isdigit(c) && c != '.')
        return c;                     /* not a number         */
    i = 0;
    if (isdigit(c))                   /* collect integer part */
        while (isdigit(s[++i] = c = line[li++]))
            ;
    if (c == '.')                     /* collect fraction part */
        while (isdigit(s[++i] = c = line[li++]))
            ;
    s[i] = '\0';
    li--;
    return NUMBER;
}
```

Instead of using `getch` and `ungetch` we use `getline` in the function `getop`. `line` is an array that contains one entire input line at a time; `li` is the index for the next character in `line`. We made `line` and `li` external variables so that they will maintain their values between calls, unlike local variables.

If `getop` is at the end of the line (or we do not have a line yet)

```
if (line[li] == '\0')
```

then `getop` invokes `getline` to get a line.

In the original `getop` (page 78 K&R) the function invokes `getch` every time it needs another character. In this version we get the character at position `li`, in `line`, and then we increment `li`. At the end of the function, instead of calling `ungetch` to push a character back, we decrement `li` because we went one character too far.

Remember that any function may use and modify external variables in another function, so `li` and `line` could be modified by a function other than `getop`. Sometimes we want to prevent this from happening so we should declare the variables to be `static`. We did not do so because `static` variables are not discussed until page 83 K&R.

Exercise 4-11: (page 83 K&R)

Modify getop so that it doesn't need to use ungetch. Hint: use an internal static variable.

```
#include  <stdio.h>
#include  <ctype.h>

#define  NUMBER  '0'  /* signal that a number was found  */

int getch(void);

/* getop: get next operator or numeric operand            */
int getop(char s[])
{
    int c, i;
    static int lastc = 0;

    if (lastc == 0)
        c = getch();
    else {
        c = lastc;
        lastc = 0;
    }
    while ((s[0] = c) == ' ' || c == '\t')
        c = getch();
    s[1] = '\0';
    if (!isdigit(c) && c != '.')
        return c;                       /* not a number       */
    i = 0;
    if (isdigit(c))                     /* collect integer part */
        while (isdigit(s[++i] = c = getch()))
            ;
    if (c == '.')                       /* collect fraction part */
        while (isdigit(s[++i] = c = getch()))
            ;
    s[i] = '\0';
    if (c != EOF)
        lastc = c;
    return NUMBER;
}
```

We modified getop to have an internal static variable that remembers the last character that we should push back onto the input. Since we do not use ungetch we store the character in lastc.

When `getop` is invoked it checks for a previous character in `lastc`. If one does not exist the function invokes `getch` to get a new character. If there is a previous character then `getop` copies the character into `c` and zeros out `lastc`. The first `while` statement changed a bit. The reason is that `getop` needs to get another character only after it examines the current character in `c`.

Exercise 4-12: (page 88 K&R)

Adapt the ideas of `printd` to write a recursive version of `itoa`; that is, convert an integer into a string by calling a recursive routine.

```
#include  <math.h>

/* itoa: convert n to characters in s; recursive        */
void itoa(int n, char s[])
{
     static int i;

     if (n / 10)
          itoa(n / 10, s);
     else {
          i = 0;
          if (n < 0)
               s[i++] = '-';
     }
     s[i++] = abs(n) % 10 + '0';
     s[i]   = '\0';
}
```

`itoa` receives two arguments: an integer `n` and array of characters `s`. If the result of the integer division `n/10` is not zero then `itoa` calls itself with `n/10`:

```
if (n / 10)
  itoa(n / 10, s);
```

When `n/10` is zero in one of the recursive calls we are looking at the most significant (leftmost) digit in `n`. We use a `static` variable `i` as the index for the array `s`. If `n` is negative we put a minus sign in the first position of the array `s` and increment `i`. As `itoa` returns from the recursive calls it calculates the digits from left to right. Note that each level adds a `'\0'` to terminate the string and the next level overwrites the `'\0'`, except the last.

Exercise 4-13: (page 88 K&R)

Write a recursive version of the function `reverse(s)`, which reverses the string
`s` in place.

```
#include <string.h>

/* reverse: reverse string s in place                          */
void reverse(char s[])
{
     void reverser(char s[], int i, int len);

     reverser(s, 0, strlen(s));
}

/* reverser: reverse string s in place; recursive             */
void reverser(char s[], int i, int len)
{
     int c, j;

     j = len - (i + 1);
     if (i < j) {
          c = s[i];
          s[i] = s[j];
          s[j] = c;
          reverser(s, ++i, len);
     }
}
```

    We need to maintain the same user interface to the routine `reverse`
regardless of implementation.   Therefore, we pass only the character string to
`reverse`.
    `reverse` determines the length of the string and then calls `reverser`,
which reverses the string `s` in place.
    `reverser` receives three arguments: `s` is the string to be reversed, `i` is
the left-side index for the string, and `len` is the length of the string (`strlen(s)`,
page 39 K&R).
    Initially, `i` is equal to 0.   `j` is the right-side index for the string.   `j` is
computed as

```
j = len - (i + 1);
```

    The characters in the string are swapped from the outside in. For example,
the first two characters swapped are `s[0]` and `s[len-1]` and the second two

characters swapped are s[1] and s[len-2].   The left-side index, i, is incremented by 1, every time reverser is called:

```
reverser(s, ++i, len);
```

The swapping continues until either the two indexes are pointing to the same characters (i == j) or the left-side index points to a character to the right of the right-side index (i > j).

This is not a good application of recursion.   Certain problems lend themselves to recursive solutions—see, for example, the function treeprint on page 142 K&R.   Other problems are best solved without recursion.   This is one of them.

Exercise 4-14: (page 91 K&R)

Define a macro swap(t,x,y) that interchanges two arguments of type t. (Block structure will help.)

```
#define    swap(t, x, y)  {    t _z;   \
                               _z = y;  \
                               y = x;   \
                               x = _z; }
```

We use the braces to define a new block. At the beginning of a block we can declare local variables. _z is a local variable of type t that helps swap the two arguments.

The swap macro works if neither of the arguments is _z. If one of the arguments has the name _z,

```
swap(int, _z, x);
```

then when the macro is expanded, it becomes

```
{ int _z; _z = _z; _z = x; x = _z; }
```

and the two arguments are not swapped. The assumption is that _z will not be used as a variable name.

Exercise 5-1: (page 97 K&R)

As written, get int treats a + or - not followed by a digit as a valid representation of zero.   Fix it to push such a character back on the input.

```c
#include  <stdio.h>
#include  <ctype.h>

int getch(void);
void ungetch(int);

/* getint: get next integer from input into *pn           */
int getint(int *pn)
{
    int c, d, sign;

    while (isspace(c = getch()))  /* skip white space      */
        ;
    if (!isdigit(c) && c != EOF && c != '+' && c != '-') {
        ungetch(c);                /* it's not a number     */
        return 0;
    }
    sign = (c == '-') ? -1 : 1;
    if (c == '+' || c == '-') {
        d = c;                     /* remember sign char    */
        if(!isdigit(c = getch())) {
            if (c != EOF)
                ungetch(c);        /* push back non-digit   */
            ungetch(d);            /* push back sign char   */
            return d;              /* return sign char      */
        }
    }
```

```
    for (*pn = 0; isdigit(c); c = getch())
         *pn = 10 * *pn + (c - '0');
    *pn *= sign;
    if (c != EOF)
         ungetch(c);
    return c;
}
```

When there is a sign character, getint saves it in d and gets the next character. If the next character is not a digit and it is not EOF, getint pushes it back on the input. Then the function pushes back the sign character and returns the sign character to indicate this situation.

Exercise 5-2: (page 97 K&R)

Write `getfloat`, the floating-point analog of `getint`. What type does `get-float` return as its function value?

```
#include  <stdio.h>
#include  <ctype.h>

int getch(void);
void ungetch(int);

/* getfloat: get next floating-point number from input       */
int getfloat(float *pn)
{
    int c, sign;
    float power;

    while (isspace(c = getch()))        /* skip white space */
        ;
    if (!isdigit(c) && c != EOF && c != '+' &&
        c != '-' && c != '.') {
        ungetch(c);                      /* it's not a number*/
        return 0;
    }
    sign = (c == '-') ? -1 : 1;
    if (c == '+' || c == '-')
        c = getch();
    for (*pn = 0.0; isdigit(c); c = getch())
        *pn = 10.0 * *pn + (c - '0'); /* integer part     */
    if (c == '.')
        c = getch();
    for (power = 1.0; isdigit(c); c = getch()) {
        *pn = 10.0 * *pn + (c - '0'); /* fractional part  */
        power *= 10.0;
    }
    *pn *= sign / power;                 /* final number     */
    if (c != EOF)
        ungetch(c);
    return c;
}
```

The routine `getfloat` is similar to the routine `getint` (page 97 K&R). `getfloat` skips white spaces, records the sign, and stores the integer part of the number at the address in `pn`.

`getfloat` also handles the fractional part of the number (but not scientific notation).   The fractional part is added to `*pn` in the same fashion as the integer part:

```
*pn = 10.0 * *pn + (c - '0');
```

For each digit collected after the decimal point the variable `power` is multiplied by 10.   For example, if 0 digits follow the decimal point `power` equals 1, if 1 digit follows the decimal point `power` equals 10, and if 3 digits follow the decimal point `power` equals 1000.

And then `getfloat` multiplies the final value of `*pn` by `sign/power` to get the floating-point value.

The function returns either `EOF` or the ASCII value of the first character after the floating-point number.   The function type is `int`.

Exercise 5-3: (page 107 K&R)

Write a pointer version of the function `strcat` that we showed in Chapter 2: `strcat(s,t)` copies the string t to the end of s.

```
/* strcat: concatenate t to the end of s; pointer version  */
void strcat(char *s, char *t)
{
    while (*s)
        s++;
    while (*s++ = *t++)
        ;
}
```

Initially s and t point to the beginning of the character strings.

The first `while` loop increments the pointer s until it finds the end of string marker (`'\0'`). The statement

```
while (*s)
```

is true as long as the character is not the end of the string marker.

The second `while` loop appends the string t to the string s:

```
while (*s++ = *t++)
    ;
```

The above statement assigns to `*s` whatever is in `*t`, increments both pointers, and continues as long as t does not point to the end of string marker.

Exercise 5-4: (page 107 K&R)

Write the function strend(s,t), which returns 1 if the string t occurs at the
end of the string s, and zero otherwise.

```
/* strend: return 1 if string t occurs at the end of s      */
int strend(char *s, char *t)
{
    char *bs = s;                  /* remember beginning of strs */
    char *bt = t;

    for ( ; *s; s++)               /* end of the string s         */
        ;
    for ( ; *t; t++)               /* end of the string t         */
        ;
    for ( ; *s == *t; s--, t--)
        if (t == bt || s == bs)
            break;                 /* at the beginning of a str   */
    if (*s == *t && t == bt && *s != '\0')
        return 1;
    else
        return 0;
}
```

We save the beginning addresses of the strings in the pointers bs and bt
and then we find the end of each string as we did in strcat. To determine if
the string t occurs at the end of the string s we start comparing the last character
in s with the last character in t and move toward the beginning of the strings.
   strend returns 1 (the string t occurs at the end of the string s) when the
characters in t match the characters in s, the pointer t is back at the beginning
of the string, and the strings are not empty:

```
if (*s == *t && t == bt && *s != '\0')
    return 1;
```

Exercise 5-5: (page 107 K&R)

Write the versions of the library functions `strncpy`, `strncat`, and `strncmp`, which operate on at most the first n characters of their argument strings. For example, `strncpy(s,t,n)` copies at most n characters of t to s. Full descriptions are in Appendix B (page 249 K&R).

```
/* strncpy: copy n characters from t to s                     */
void strncpy(char *s, char *t, int n)
{
    while (*t && n-- > 0)
        *s++ = *t++;
    while (n-- > 0)
        *s++ = '\0';
}

/* strncat: concatenate n characters of t to the end of s    */
void strncat(char *s, char *t, int n)
{
    void strncpy(char *s, char *t, int n);
    int strlen(char *);

    strncpy(s+strlen(s), t, n);
}

/* strncmp: compare at most n characters of t with s          */
int strncmp(char *s, char *t, int n)
{
    for ( ; *s == *t; s++, t++)
        if (*s == '\0' || --n <= 0)
            return 0;
    return *s - *t;
}
```

The functions `strncpy` and `strncat` have the type void as `strcpy` on page 105 K&R. The library versions of these functions return a pointer to the beginning of the target string.

`strncpy` copies at most n characters from t to s. If t has less than n characters we pad the string s with '\0'.

`strncat` invokes `strncpy` to copy at most n characters from the string t starting at the end of the string s.

`strncmp` compares at most n characters of t with characters of s. The function is similar to `strcmp` on page 106 K&R. This time we terminate the comparison when we find the end of the strings or we successfully compare n characters:

```
if (*s == '\0' || --n <= 0)
    return 0;
```

Exercise 5-6: (page 107 K&R)

Rewrite appropriate programs from earlier chapters and exercises with pointers instead of array indexing. Good possibilities include getline (Chapters 1 and 4), atoi, itoa, and their variants (Chapters 2, 3, and 4), reverse (Chapter 3), and strindex and getop (Chapter 4).

```
#include  <stdio.h>

/* getline: read a line into s, return length                 */
int getline(char *s, int lim)
{
    int c;
    char *t = s;

    while (--lim > 0 && (c=getchar()) != EOF && c != '\n')
        *s++ = c;
    if (c == '\n')
        *s++ = c;
    *s = '\0';
    return s - t;
}
```

getline receives a pointer to an array of characters. We use *s instead of s[i] to refer to an element in the array and we increment the pointer s to travel down the array.

The statement

```
s[i++] = c;
```

is equivalent to

```
*s++ = c;
```

At the beginning of the function, s points to the beginning of the array and we save that address in the pointer t:

```
char *t = s;
```

After getline reads a line, s points to the terminating character ('\0'). t still points to the first character in the line so the length of the line is s-t.

```
#include  <ctype.h>

/* atoi: convert s to integer; pointer version                */
int atoi(char *s)
{
```

```
    int  n,  sign;

    for  (  ;  isspace(*s);  s++)                    /*  skip  white  space  */
        ;
    sign  =  (*s  ==  '-')  ?  -1  :  1;
    if  (*s  ==  '+'  ||  *s  ==  '-')              /*  skip  sign          */
        s++;
    for  (n  =  0;  isdigit(*s);  s++)
        n  =  10  *  n  +  *s  -  '0';
    return  sign  *  n;
}
```

s[i] is equivalent to *s. s[i++] is equivalent to *s++.

```
void  reverse(char  *);

/*  itoa:  convert  n  to  characters  in  s;  pointer  version    */
void  itoa(int  n,  char  *s)
{
    int  sign;
    char  *t  =  s;                          /*  save  pointer  to  s    */

    if  ((sign  =  n)  <  0)                  /*  record  sign            */
        n  =  -n;                            /*  make  n  positive        */
    do  {                        /*  generate  digits  in  reverse  order*/
        *s++  =  n  %  10  +  '0';        /*  get  next  digit          */
    }  while  ((n  /=  10)  >  0);          /*  delete  it              */
    if  (sign  <  0)
        *s++  =  '-';
    *s  =  '\0';
    reverse(t);
}
```

The character pointer t is initialized to point to the first element in the string s:

```
char  *t  =  s;
```

The statement

```
*s++  =  n  %  10  +  '0';
```

is equivalent to

```
s[i++]  =  n  %  10  +  '0';
```

We invoke `reverse` with a pointer to the beginning of the string `s`.

```
#include  <string.h>

/* reverse: reverse string s in place                           */
void reverse(char *s)
{
    int c;
    char *t;

    for (t = s + (strlen(s)-1); s < t; s++, t--) {
        c = *s;
        *s = *t;
        *t = c;
    }
}
```

`s` points to the first character of the string and we set the character pointer
`t` to point to the last character of the string (excluding the terminating `'\0'`):

```
t = s + (strlen(s)-1)
```

`*s` is equivalent to `s[i]` and `*t` is equivalent to `s[j]`. The test in the
`for` loop

```
s < t
```

is equivalent to the test

```
i < j
```

`s++` has the same effect as incrementing the index `i` (`i++`) and `t--` has
the same effect as decrementing the index `j` (`j--`).

```
/* strindex: return index of t in s, -1 if none                 */
int strindex(char *s, char *t)
{
    char *b = s;                    /* beginning of string s */
    char *p, *r;

    for (; *s != '\0'; s++) {
        for (p=s, r=t; *r != '\0' && *p == *r; p++, r++)
            ;
        if (r > t && *r == '\0')
            return s - b;
    }
    return -1;
}
```

s[i] is replaced by *s, s[j] is replaced by *p, and t[k] is replaced by
*r. b is a character pointer that always points to the first element of the string
s (s[0]). p = s is equivalent to j = i. r = t is equivalent to k = 0.

When the if statement is true

```
if (r > t && *r == '\0')
```

a match exists and strindex returns the index of t in the string s:

```
return s - b;
```

```
#include  <ctype.h>

/* atof: convert string s to double; pointer version       */
double atof(char *s)
{
      double val, power;
      int sign;

      for ( ; isspace(*s); s++)       /* skip white space   */
          ;
      sign = (*s == '-') ? -1 : 1;
      if (*s == '+' || *s == '-')
          s++;
      for (val = 0.0; isdigit(*s); s++)
          val = 10.0 * val + (*s - '0');
      if (*s == '.')
          s++;
      for (power = 1.0; isdigit(*s); s++) {
          val = 10.0 * val + (*s - '0');
          power *= 10.0;
      }
      return sign * val / power;
}
```

s[i++] is equivalent to *s++.

```
#include   <stdio.h>
#include   <ctype.h>

#define    NUMBER    '0'   /* signal that a number was found  */

int getch(void);
void ungetch(int);

/* getop: get next operator or numeric operand; pointer ver */
int getop(char *s)
{
    int c;

    while ((*s = c = getch()) == ' ' || c == '\t')
        ;
    *(s+1) = '\0';
    if (!isdigit(c) && c != '.')
        return c;                    /* not a number         */
    if (isdigit(c))                  /* collect integer part */
        while (isdigit(*++s = c = getch()))
            ;
    if (c == '.')                    /* collect fraction part */
        while (isdigit(*++s = c = getch()))
            ;
    *s = '\0';
    if (c != EOF)
        ungetch(c);
    return NUMBER;
}
```

We use pointers to replace references to array elements. The changes are straightforward. Instead of

```
s[1] = '\0';
```

we use

```
*(s+1) = '\0';
```

to place an end of string marker at the second position of the array without changing the pointer.

Exercise 5-7: (page 110 K&R)

Rewrite `readlines` to store lines in an array supplied by `main`, rather than calling `alloc` to maintain storage. How much faster is the program?

```
#include  <string.h>

#define   MAXLEN     1000 /* maximum length of line          */
#define   MAXSTOR    5000 /* size of available storage space */

int getline(char *, int);

/* readlines: read input lines                              */
int readlines(char *lineptr[], char *linestor, int maxlines)
{
    int len, nlines;
    char line[MAXLEN];
    char *p = linestor;
    char *linestop = linestor + MAXSTOR;

    nlines = 0;
    while ((len = getline(line, MAXLEN)) > 0)
        if (nlines >= maxlines || p+len > linestop)
            return -1;
        else {
            line[len-1] = '\0';        /* delete newline    */
            strcpy(p, line);
            lineptr[nlines++] = p;
            p += len;
        }
    return nlines;
}
```

The main routine supplies the array `linestor` where `readlines` stores the text for the lines. The character pointer `p` is initialized to point to the first element of `linestor`:

```
char *p = linestor;
```

The original routine `readlines` (page 109 K&R) uses the routine `alloc` (page 101 K&R):

```
if ((nlines >= maxlines || (p = alloc(len)) == NULL)
```

In this version `readlines` stores `line` in `linestor` starting at position p. The statement

```
if (nlines >= maxlines !! p+len > linestop)
```

ensures that there is available space in `linestor`.

This version of `readlines` is slightly faster than the original one.

Exercise 5-8: (page 112 K&R)

There is no error checking in `day_of_year` or `month_day`. Remedy this defect.

```
static char daytab[2][13] = {
    {0, 31, 28, 31, 30, 31, 30, 31, 31, 30, 31, 30, 31},
    {0, 31, 29, 31, 30, 31, 30, 31, 31, 30, 31, 30, 31}
};

/* day_of_year: set day of year from month & day          */
int day_of_year(int year, int month, int day)
{
    int i, leap;

    leap = year%4 == 0 && year%100 != 0 || year%400 == 0;
    if (month < 1 || month > 12)
        return -1;
    if (day < 1 || day > daytab[leap][month])
        return -1;
    for (i = 1; i < month; i++)
        day += daytab[leap][i];
    return day;
}


/* month_day: set month, day from day of year             */
void month_day(int year, int yearday, int *pmonth, int *pday)
{
    int i, leap;

    if (year < 1) {
        *pmonth = -1;
        *pday = -1;
        return;
    }
    leap = year%4 == 0 && year%100 != 0 || year%400 == 0;
    for (i = 1; i <= 12 && yearday > daytab[leap][i]; i++)
        yearday -= daytab[leap][i];
    if (i > 12 && yearday > daytab[leap][12]) {
        *pmonth = -1;
        *pday = -1;
    } else {
        *pmonth = i;
        *pday = yearday;
    }
}
```

In `day_of_year` we check for reasonable values in `month` and `day`. If `month` is less than one or greater than twelve, `day_of_year` returns −1. If `day` is less than one or `day` exceeds the number of days for the month, the function returns −1.

In `month_day` we first check for negative `year`. You may want to add this kind of check in `day_of_year` also. Then we proceed to decrement `yearday` while we check that the month (index `i`) does not exceed 12. If the loop terminates with month 13 and the value in `yearday` exceeds the number of days in the last month of the year, then `yearday` started with an incorrect value and we set both month and day to −1. Otherwise the function `month_day` received correct values.

Exercise 5-9: (page 114 K&R)

Rewrite the routines `day_of_year` and `month_day` with pointers instead of indexing.

```
static char daytab[2][13] = {
    {0, 31, 28, 31, 30, 31, 30, 31, 31, 30, 31, 30, 31},
    {0, 31, 29, 31, 30, 31, 30, 31, 31, 30, 31, 30, 31}
};

/* day_of_year: set day of year from month & day        */
int day_of_year(int year, int month, int day)
{
    int leap;
    char *p;

    leap = year%4 == 0 && year%100 != 0 || year%400 == 0;
    p = daytab[leap];
    while (--month)
        day += *++p;
    return day;
}


/* month_day: set month, day from day of year           */
void month_day(int year, int yearday, int *pmonth, int *pday)
{
    int leap;
    char *p;

    leap = year%4 == 0 && year%100 != 0 || year%400 == 0;
    p = daytab[leap];
    while (yearday > *++p)
        yearday -= *p;
    *pmonth = p - *(daytab + leap);
    *pday = yearday;
}
```

`p` points to the first or second row of `daytab` depending on the value of `leap`:

```
p = daytab[leap];
```

The `for` loop in the original `day_of_year` routine

```
for (i = 1; i < month; i++)
    day += daytab[leap][i];
```

is equivalent to the while loop

```
while (--month)
     day += *++p;
```

in the revised day_of_year routine.
    The for loop in the original month_day routine

```
for (i = 1; yearday > daytab[leap][i]; i++)
     yearday -= daytab[leap][i];
```

is equivalent to the statements

```
p = daytab[leap];
while (yearday > *++p)
     yearday -= *p;
```

in the revised month_day routine.

Exercise 5-10: (page 118 K&R)

Write the program `expr`, which evaluates a reverse Polish expression from the command line, where each operator or operand is a separate argument. For example,

```
expr 2   3   4   +   *
```

evaluates $2 \times (3+4)$.

```c
#include  <stdio.h>
#include  <math.h>        /* for atof()                      */

#define   MAXOP    100   /* max size of operand or operator */
#define   NUMBER   '0'   /* signal that a number was found  */

int getop(char []);
void ungets(char []);
void push(double);
double pop(void);

/* reverse Polish calculator; uses command line            */
main(int argc, char *argv[])
{
    char s[MAXOP];
    double op2;

    while (--argc > 0) {
        ungets(" ");              /* push end of argument   */
        ungets(*++argv);          /* push an argument       */
        switch (getop(s)) {
        case NUMBER:
            push(atof(s));
            break;
        case '+':
            push(pop() + pop());
            break;
        case '*':
            push(pop() * pop());
            break;
        case '-':
            op2 = pop();
            push(pop() - op2);
            break;
```

```
        case '/':
            op2 = pop();
            if (op2 != 0.0)
                push(pop() / op2);
            else
                printf("error: zero divisor\n");
            break;
        default:
            printf("error: unknown command %s\n", s);
            argc = 1;
            break;
        }
    }
    printf("\t%.8g\n", pop());
    return 0;
}
```

This solution is based on the reverse Polish calculator on page 76 K&R. It uses the routines push and pop (page 77 K&R).

We use ungets to push an end of argument marker and an argument onto the input buffer. This way we can use getop unchanged. getop invokes getch to read characters and gets the next operator or numeric operand.

If an error should occur while reading in the arguments, argc is set to 1. The while loop in the main routine

```
while (--argc > 0)
```

becomes false and the program ends.

The result for a valid expression is on top of the stack and we print this result when the argument list terminates.

Exercise 5-11: (page 118 K&R)

Modify the programs entab and detab (written as exercises in Chapter 1) to
accept a list of tab stops as arguments. Use the default tab settings if there are
no arguments.

```
#include   <stdio.h>

#define    MAXLINE   100        /* maximum line size       */
#define    TABINC    8          /* default tab increment size */
#define    YES       1
#define    NO        0

void settab(int argc, char *argv[], char *tab);
void entab(char *tab);
int tabpos(int pos, char *tab);

/* replace strings of blanks with tabs                     */
main(int argc, char *argv[])
{
    char tab[MAXLINE+1];

    settab(argc, argv, tab);      /* initialize tab stops */
    entab(tab);                   /* replace blanks w/ tab */
    return 0;
}

/* entab: replace strings of blanks with tabs and blanks   */
void entab(char *tab)
{
    int c, pos;
    int nb = 0;                      /* # of blanks necessary */
    int nt = 0;                      /* # of tabs necessary   */

    for (pos = 1; (c=getchar()) != EOF; pos++)
        if (c == ' ') {
            if (tabpos(pos, tab) == NO)
                ++nb;                /* increment # of blanks */
            else {
                nb = 0;              /* reset # of blanks     */
                ++nt;                /* one more tab          */
            }
```

```
        } else {
            for ( ; nt > 0; nt--)
                putchar('\t'); /* output tab(s)           */
            if (c == '\t')        /* forget the blank(s)     */
                nb = 0;
            else                  /* output blank(s)         */
                for ( ; nb > 0; nb--)
                    putchar(' ');
            putchar(c);
            if (c == '\n')
                pos = 0;
            else if (c == '\t')
                while (tabpos(pos, tab) != YES)
                    ++pos;
        }
}
```

The source file settab.c:

```
#include  <stdlib.h>

#define   MAXLINE  100      /* maximum line size          */
#define   TABINC   8        /* default tab increment size */
#define   YES      1
#define   NO       0

/* settab: set tab stops in array tab                     */
void settab(int argc, char *argv[], char *tab)
{
    int i, pos;

    if (argc <= 1)           /* default tab stops          */
        for (i = 1; i <= MAXLINE; i++)
            if (i % TABINC == 0)
                tab[i] = YES;
            else
                tab[i] = NO;
    else {                   /* user provided tab stops    */
        for (i = 1; i <= MAXLINE; i++)
            tab[i] = NO;   /* turn off all tab stops     */
        while (--argc > 0) {/* walk through argument list */
            pos = atoi(*++argv);
            if (pos > 0 && pos <= MAXLINE)
                tab[pos] = YES;
        }
    }
}
```

The source file `tabpos.c`:

```
#define    MAXLINE    100         /* maximum line size          */
#define    YES        1

/* tabpos: determine if pos is at a tab stop                    */
int tabpos(int pos, char *tab)
{
      if (pos > MAXLINE)
           return YES;
      else
           return tab[pos];
}
```

The framework for this solution is the `entab` program in Kernighan & Plauger, *Software Tools* (Addison-Wesley, 1976).

Each element in the array `tab` corresponds to a position within the line, i.e., `tab[1]` corresponds to the first position within the line (`pos` equals 1). If the position is a tab stop, then the corresponding element `tab[i]` equals `YES`; otherwise `tab[i]` equals `NO`.

The tab stops are initialized in the routine `settab`. If there are no arguments (`argc` equals 1), then we put a tab stop every `TABINC` position.

If there are arguments, then we set the tab stops as the user specifies them.

The routine `entab` is similar to Exercise 1-21.

The routine `tabpos` determines if the position is a tab stop. It returns `YES` if `pos` exceeds `MAXLINE`, otherwise it returns `tab[pos]`.

```
#include   <stdio.h>

#define    MAXLINE    100         /* maximum line size          */
#define    TABINC     8           /* default tab increment size */
#define    YES        1
#define    NO         0

void settab(int argc, char *argv[], char *tab);
void detab(char *tab);
int tabpos(int pos, char *tab);

/* replace tabs with blanks                                     */
main(int argc, char *argv[])
{
      char tab[MAXLINE+1];

      settab(argc, argv, tab);          /* initialize tab stops  */
      detab(tab);                       /* replace tab w/ blanks */
      return 0;
}
```

```
/* detab: replace tab with blanks                            */
void detab(char *tab)
{
    int c, pos = 1;

    while ((c = getchar()) != EOF)
        if (c == '\t') {              /* tab character        */
            do
                putchar(' ');
            while (tabpos(pos++, tab) != YES);
        } else if (c == '\n') {   /* newline character    */
            putchar(c);
            pos = 1;
        } else {                      /* all other characters */
            putchar(c);
            ++pos;
        }
}
```

The framework for this solution is the detab program in Kernighan &
Plauger, *Software Tools* (Addison-Wesley, 1976).
    The routines tabpos and settab are the same as in the first part of this
exercise.
    The routine detab is similar to Exercise 1-20.

Exercise 5-12: (page 118 K&R)

Extend `entab` and `detab` to accept the shorthand

```
entab -m +n
```

to mean tab stops every *n* columns, starting at column *m*.   Choose convenient (for the user) default behavior.

```
#include  <stdio.h>

#define    MAXLINE    100         /* maximum line size        */
#define    TABINC     8           /* default tab increment size */
#define    YES        1
#define    NO         0

void esettab(int argc, char *argv[], char *tab);
void entab(char *tab);

/* replace strings of blanks with tabs                        */
main(int argc, char *argv[])
{
     char tab[MAXLINE+1];

     esettab(argc, argv, tab);    /* initialize tab stops */
     entab(tab);                  /* replace blanks w/ tab */
     return 0;
}
```

     The source file `esettab.c`:

```
#include  <stdlib.h>

#define    MAXLINE    100         /* maximum line size        */
#define    TABINC     8           /* default tab increment size */
#define    YES        1
#define    NO         0

/* esettab: set tab stops in array tab                        */
void esettab(int argc, char *argv[], char *tab)
{
     int i, inc, pos;
```

```
    if (argc <= 1)              /* default tab stops        */
        for (i = 1; i <= MAXLINE; i++)
            if (i % TABINC == 0)
                tab[i] = YES;
            else
                tab[i] = NO;
    else if (argc == 3 &&    /* user provided range          */
            *argv[1] == '-' && *argv[2] == '+') {
        pos = atoi(&(*++argv)[1]);
        inc = atoi(&(*++argv)[1]);
        for (i = 1; i <= MAXLINE; i++)
            if (i != pos)
                tab[i] = NO;
            else {
                tab[i] = YES;
                pos += inc;
            }
    } else {                    /* user provided tab stops    */
        for (i = 1; i <= MAXLINE; i++)
            tab[i] = NO;    /* turn off all tab stops       */
        while (--argc > 0) {/* walk through argument list */
            pos = atoi(*++argv);
            if (pos > 0 && pos <= MAXLINE)
                tab[pos] = YES;
        }
    }
}
```

The framework for this solution is the entab program in Kernighan & Plauger, *Software Tools* (Addison-Wesley, 1976).

This solution is similar to the entab program in Exercise 5-11. The only modification is that the routine settab was replaced by esettab (extended settab).

esettab accepts the shorthand notation $-m\ +n$. The statements

```
pos = atoi(&(*++argv)[1]);
inc = atoi(&(*++argv)[1]);
```

set pos equal to the first tab stop and set inc equal to the increment size. Therefore, the tab stops begin at pos and occur at every inc position.

```
#include    <stdio.h>

#define    MAXLINE    100       /* maximum line size         */
#define    TABINC     8         /* default tab increment size */
#define    YES        1
#define    NO         0

void esettab(int argc, char *argv[], char *tab);
void detab(char *tab);

/* replace tabs with blanks                                  */
main(int argc, char *argv[])
{
     char tab[MAXLINE+1];

     esettab(argc, argv, tab);     /* initialize tab stops  */
     detab(tab);                   /* replace tab w/ blanks */
     return 0;
}
```

The framework for this solution is the detab program in Kernighan & Plauger, *Software Tools* (Addison-Wesley, 1976).

This solution is similar to the detab program in Exercise 5-11 and uses the routine esettab from the first part of this exercise.

Exercise 5-13: (page 118 K&R)

Write the program tail, which prints the last *n* lines of its input. By default, *n* is 10, let us say, but it can be changed by an optional argument, so that

```
tail -n
```

prints the last *n* lines. The program should behave rationally no matter how unreasonable the input or the value of *n*. Write the program so that it makes the best use of available storage; lines should be stored as in the sorting program of Section 5.6, not in a two-dimensional array of fixed size.

```c
#include    <stdio.h>
#include    <stdlib.h>
#include    <string.h>

#define     DEFLINES  10   /* default # of lines to print    */
#define     LINES     100  /* max # of lines to print        */
#define     MAXLEN    100  /* max length of an input line    */

void error(char *);
int getline(char *, int);

/* print last n lines of the input                           */
main(int argc, char *argv[])
{
    char *p;
    char *buf;                /* pointer to large buffer      */
    char *bufend;             /* end of the buffer            */
    char line[MAXLEN];        /* current input line           */
    char *lineptr[LINES];     /* pointers to lines read       */
    int first, i, last, len, n, nlines;

    if (argc == 1)            /* no argument present          */
        n = DEFLINES;         /* use default # of lines       */
    else if (argc == 2 && (*++argv)[0] == '-')
        n = atoi(argv[0]+1);
    else
        error("usage:  tail [-n]");
    if (n < 1 || n > LINES)   /* unreasonable value for n?    */
        n = LINES;
    for (i = 0; i < LINES; i++)
        lineptr[i] = NULL;
    if ((p = buf = malloc(LINES * MAXLEN)) == NULL)
        error("tail: cannot allocate buf");
    bufend = buf + LINES * MAXLEN;
    last = 0;                 /* index of last line read      */
    nlines = 0;               /* number of lines read         */
```

```
    while ((len = getline(line, MAXLEN)) > 0) {
        if (p + len + 1 >= bufend)
            p = buf;        /* buffer wrap around          */
        lineptr[last] = p;
        strcpy(lineptr[last], line);
        if (++last >= LINES)
            last = 0;        /* ptrs to buffer wrap around */
        p += len + 1;
        nlines++;
    }
    if (n > nlines)                /* req. lines more than rec.? */
        n = nlines;
    first = last - n;
    if (first < 0)                 /* it did wrap around the list*/
        first += LINES;
    for (i = first; n-- > 0; i = (i + 1) % LINES)
        printf("%s", lineptr[i]);
    return 0;
}

/* error: print error message and exit                          */
void error(char *s)
{
    printf("%s\n", s);
    exit(1);
}
```

The program prints the last *n* lines of its input. When argc is 1, *n* has the default value DEFLINES. When argc is 2, the value for *n* is obtained from the command line. It is an error for argc to be greater than 2.

The loop

```
while ((len = getline(line, MAXLEN)) > 0)
```

gets a line at a time until getline (Exercise 1-16) finds the end of its input. For each line read the program uses space in the allocated buffer.

The statement

```
if (p + len + 1 >= bufend)
    p = buf;
```

resets the pointer p to the beginning of the buffer when there is not enough room left to copy the current line.

The elements of the array lineptr point to characters: the last LINES lines read so far. The index for this array is the variable last.

When last becomes equal to LINES it wraps around and the elements of lineptr and their buffers are then reused.

The total number of lines is `nlines`. The program prints the last *n* lines, so the number of lines requested cannot exceed the number of lines received:

```
if (n > nlines)
    n = nlines;
```

If the total number of lines exceeds `LINES`, the index `last` wraps around and the starting index has to be adjusted:

```
if (first < 0)
    first += LINES;
```

The program then prints the last *n* lines:

```
for (i = first; n-- > 0; i = (i + 1) % LINES)
    printf("%s", lineptr[i]);
```

Since `i` starts with the value of `first` and goes for *n* elements, it may wrap around. The modulus (remainder) operator maintains `i` between the values 0 and `LINES-1`:

```
i = (i + 1) % LINES
```

The standard library function `exit` (page 163 K&R) terminates the program when an error occurs. `exit` returns 1 indicating an error condition.

Exercise 5-14: (page 121 K&R)

Modify the sort program to handle a -r flag, which indicates sorting in reverse
(decreasing) order. Be sure that -r works with -n.

```
#include <stdio.h>
#include <string.h>

#define    NUMERIC    1      /* numeric sort                    */
#define    DECR       2      /* sort in decreasing order        */
#define    LINES      100    /* max # of lines to be sorted     */

int numcmp(char *, char *);
int readlines(char *lineptr[], int maxlines);
void qsort(char *v[], int left, int right,
           int (*comp)(void *, void *));
void writelines(char *lineptr[], int nlines, int decr);

static char option = 0;

/* sort input lines  */
main(int argc, char *argv[])
{
    char *lineptr[LINES];       /* pointers to text lines    */
    int nlines;                 /* number of input lines read */
    int c, rc = 0;

    while (--argc > 0 && (*++argv)[0] == '-')
        while (c = *++argv[0])
            switch (c) {
            case 'n' :      /* numeric sort                 */
                option != NUMERIC;
                break;
            case 'r':       /* sort in decreasing order     */
                option != DECR;
                break;
            default:
                printf("sort: illegal option %c\n", c);
                argc = 1;
                rc = -1;
                break;
            }
```

```
    if (argc)
        printf("Usage: sort -nr \n");
    else
        if ((nlines = readlines(lineptr, LINES)) > 0) {
            if (option & NUMERIC)
                qsort((void **) lineptr, 0, nlines-1,
                    (int (*) (void *, void *)) numcmp);
            else
                qsort((void **) lineptr, 0, nlines-1,
                    (int (*) (void *, void *)) strcmp);
            writelines(lineptr, nlines, option & DECR);
        } else {
            printf("input too big to sort \n");
            rc = -1;
        }
    return rc;
}


/* writelines: write output lines                          */
void writelines(char *lineptr[], int nlines, int decr)
{
    int i;

    if (decr)                      /* print in decreasing order  */
        for (i = nlines-1; i >= 0; i--)
            printf("%s\n", lineptr[i]);
    else                           /* print in increasing order  */
        for (i = 0; i < nlines; i++)
            printf("%s\n", lineptr[i]);
}
```

The bits of the static character variable option determine which options are requested.

> 0th bit = 0 character string sort
> = 1 numeric sort (-n)

> 1st bit = 0 sort in increasing order
> = 1 sort in decreasing order (-r)

If there is an option present, then the bitwise inclusive OR operator (|) sets the appropriate bit in the variable option. The statement

```
option != DECR;
```

is equivalent to

```
option = option ! 2;
```

The decimal number 2 is equivalent to 00000010 in binary.   Since

1 OR anything = 1

the above C statement sets the 1st bit in the character variable `option` to 1.
(The bits are numbered 0, 1, 2, . . . from right to left.)

To determine if an option is set we use the bitwise AND (`&`) operator.
The expression

`option & DECR`

is true if the `-r` option is requested and false if the `-r` option is not requested.

`writelines` was modified to accept a third argument, `decr`. The variable
`decr` is the result of the expression `option & DECR`, which determines whether
the sorted list is to be printed in decreasing or increasing order.

The routines `strcmp`, `numcmp`, `swap`, `qsort`, and `readlines` are those
used in the sort program (page 119 K&R).

Exercise 5-15: (page 121 K&R)

Add the option - f to fold upper and lower case together, so that case distinctions
are not made during sorting; for example, a and A compare equal.

```c
#include <stdio.h>
#include <string.h>
#include <ctype.h>

#define    NUMERIC   1      /* numeric sort                          */
#define    DECR      2      /* sort in decreasing order              */
#define    FOLD      4      /* fold upper and lower cases            */
#define    LINES     100    /* max # of lines to be sorted           */

int charcmp(char *, char *);
int numcmp(char *, char *);
int readlines(char *lineptr[], int maxlines);
void qsort(char *v[], int left, int right,
         int (*comp)(void *, void *));
void writelines(char *lineptr[], int nlines, int order);

static char option = 0;

/* sort input lines                                                  */
main(int argc, char *argv[])
{
    char *lineptr[LINES];      /* pointers to text lines      */
    int nlines;                /* number of input lines read */
    int c, rc = 0;

    while (--argc > 0 && (*++argv)[0] == '-')
        while (c = *++argv[0])
            switch (c) {
            case 'f':        /* fold upper and lower cases */
                option |= FOLD;
                break;
            case 'n':        /* numeric sort                */
                option |= NUMERIC;
                break;
            case 'r':        /* sort in decreasing order    */
                option |= DECR;
                break;
            default:
                printf("sort: illegal option %c\n", c);
                argc = 1;
                rc = -1;
                break;
            }
```

```
    if (argc)
        printf("Usage: sort -fnr \n");
    else {
        if ((nlines = readlines(lineptr, LINES)) > 0) {
            if (option & NUMERIC)
                qsort((void **) lineptr, 0, nlines-1,
                    (int (*)(void *, void *)) numcmp);
            else if (option & FOLD)
                qsort((void **) lineptr, 0, nlines-1,
                    (int (*)(void *, void *)) charcmp);
            else
                qsort((void **) lineptr, 0, nlines-1,
                    (int (*)(void *, void *)) strcmp);
            writelines(lineptr, nlines, option & DECR);
        } else {
            printf("input too big to sort \n");
            rc = -1;
        }
    }
    return rc;
}

/* charcmp: return <0 if s<t, 0 if s==t, >0 if s>t     */
int charcmp(char *s, char *t)
{
    for ( ; tolower(*s) == tolower(*t); s++, t++)
        if (*s == '\0')
            return 0;
    return tolower(*s) - tolower(*t);
}
```

The framework for this solution is Exercise 5-14.

> 2nd bit = 0 no folding
>   = 1 folding `(-f)`

If the user requests the fold option, the second bit in `option` must be set equal to 1:

```
option != FOLD;
```

FOLD (decimal 4) is 00000100 in binary (the bits are numbered 0, 1, 2, 3, . . . from right to left).

The function `charcmp` compares strings like `strcmp` (page 106 K&R). It converts characters to lower case, to support the FOLD option, and compares them.

The routines `numcmp`, `swap`, `qsort`, `readlines`, and `writelines` are those used in Exercise 5-14.

Exercise 5-16: (page 121 K&R)

Add the -d ("directory order") option, which makes comparisons only on letters, numbers, and blanks. Make sure it works in conjunction with -f.

```c
#include <stdio.h>
#include <ctype.h>

#define    NUMERIC    1      /* numeric sort                    */
#define    DECR       2      /* sort in decreasing order        */
#define    FOLD       4      /* fold upper and lower cases      */
#define    DIR        8      /* directory order                 */
#define    LINES      100    /* max # of lines to be sorted     */

int charcmp(char *, char *);
int numcmp(char *, char *);
int readlines(char *lineptr[], int maxlines);
void qsort(char *v[], int left, int right,
           int (*comp) (void *, void *));
void writelines(char *lineptr[], int nlines, int order);

static char option = 0;

/* sort input lines                                            */
main(int argc, char *argv[])
{
    char *lineptr[LINES];    /* pointers to text lines      */
    int nlines;              /* number of input lines read  */
    int c, rc = 0;

    while (--argc > 0 && (*++argv)[0] == '-')
        while (c = *++argv[0])
            switch (c) {
            case 'd':        /* directory order             */
                option != DIR;
                break;
            case 'f':        /* fold upper and lower cases */
                option != FOLD;
                break;
            case 'n':        /* numeric sort                */
                option != NUMERIC;
                break;
            case 'r':        /* sort in decreasing order    */
                option != DECR;
                break;
```

```
                        default:
                                printf("sort: illegal option %c\n", c);
                                argc = 1;
                                rc = -1;
                                break;
                        }
        if (argc)
                printf("Usage: sort -dfnr \n");
        else {
                if ((nlines = readlines(lineptr, LINES)) > 0) {
                        if (option & NUMERIC)
                                qsort((void **) lineptr, 0, nlines-1,
                                        (int (*)(void *, void *)) numcmp);
                        else
                                qsort((void **) lineptr, 0, nlines-1,
                                        (int (*)(void *, void *)) charcmp);
                        writelines(lineptr, nlines, option & DECR);
                } else {
                        printf("input too big to sort \n");
                        rc = -1;
                }
        }
        return rc;
}

/* charcmp: return <0 if s<t, 0 if s==t, >0 if s>t     */
int charcmp(char *s, char *t)
{
        char a, b;
        int fold = (option & FOLD) ? 1 : 0;
        int dir = (option & DIR) ? 1 : 0;

        do {
                if (dir) {
                        while (!isalnum(*s) && *s != ' ' && *s != '\0')
                                s++;
                        while (!isalnum(*t) && *t != ' ' && *t != '\0')
                                t++;
                }
                a = fold ? tolower(*s) : *s;
                s++;
                b = fold ? tolower(*t) : *t;
                t++;
                if (a == b && a == '\0')
                        return 0;
        } while (a == b);
        return a - b;
}
```

The framework for this solution is Exercises 5-14 and 5-15.

3rd bit   =   0 no directory order
          =   1 directory order ($-$d)

If the user requests the directory option, the third bit in `option` is set to 1.

```
option |= DIR;
```

`DIR` (decimal 8) is 00001000 in binary notation (the bits are numbered 0, 1, 2, 3, . . . from right to left).

The `charcmp` routine (Exercise 5-15) was modified to handle both the fold option and the directory option.

If the user requests the directory option then the `while` loop

```
while (!isalnum(*s) && *s != ' ' && *s != '\0')
    s++;
```

examines each character in the string `s` and skips over those characters that are not letters, numbers, and blanks. The macro `isalnum` is defined in `<ctype.h>`. `isalnum` tests for alphabetic characters (`a-z`, `A-Z`) and digits (`0-9`). If `*s` is an alphabetic character or a digit then `isalnum(*s)` is nonzero; otherwise `isalnum(*s)` is zero.

The next `while` loop

```
while (!isalnum(*t) && *t != ' ' && *t != '\0')
    t++;
```

examines each character in the string `t` and skips over those characters that are not letters, numbers, and blanks.

When a letter, number, or blank is found in `s` and a letter, number, or blank is found in `t`, the routine `charcmp` compares the two characters.

We could have taken another approach and created three functions instead of `charcmp`: `foldcmp`, `dircmp`, and `folddircmp`. `foldcmp` would fold and compare characters as `charcmp` in Exercise 5-15. `dircmp` would compare characters for directory order, and `folddircmp` would fold and compare characters for directory order. Each individual function would be faster than the current `charcmp`. We chose to complicate `charcmp` instead of creating more functions.

The routines `numcmp`, `swap`, `qsort`, `readlines`, and `writelines` are those used in Exercise 5-14.

Exercise 5-17: (page 121 K&R)

Add a field-handling capability, so sorting may be done on fields within lines, each field sorted according to an independent set of options. (The index for this book was sorted with -df for the index category and -n for the page numbers.)

```
#include <stdio.h>
#include <ctype.h>

#define   NUMERIC   1     /* numeric sort                     */
#define   DECR      2     /* sort in decreasing order         */
#define   FOLD      4     /* fold upper and lower cases       */
#define   DIR       8     /* directory order                  */
#define   LINES     100   /* max # of lines to be sorted      */

int charcmp(char *, char *);
void error(char *);
int numcmp(char *, char *);
void readargs(int argc, char *argv[]);
int readlines(char *lineptr[], int maxlines);
void qsort(char *v[], int left, int right,
          int (*comp)(void *, void *));
void writelines(char *lineptr[], int nlines, int order);

char option = 0;
int pos1 = 0;                      /* field beginning with pos1 */
int pos2 = 0;                      /* ending just before pos2   */

/* sort input lines                                            */
main(int argc, char *argv[])
{
    char *lineptr[LINES];       /* pointers to text lines      */
    int nlines;                 /* number of input lines read  */
    int rc = 0;

    readargs(argc, argv);
    if ((nlines = readlines(lineptr, LINES)) > 0) {
        if (option & NUMERIC)
            qsort((void **) lineptr, 0, nlines-1,
                (int (*)(void *, void *)) numcmp);
        else
            qsort((void **) lineptr, 0, nlines-1,
                (int (*)(void *, void *)) charcmp);
        writelines(lineptr, nlines, option & DECR);
```

```
        } else {
            printf("input too big to sort \n");
            rc = -1;
        }
        return rc;
}

/* readargs: read program arguments                        */
void readargs(int argc, char *argv[])
{
        int c;
        int atoi(char *);

        while (--argc > 0 && (c = (*++argv)[0]) == '-' || c == '+') {
            if (c == '-' && !isdigit(*(argv[0]+1)))
                while (c = *++argv[0])
                    switch (c) {
                    case 'd':       /* directory order        */
                        option |= DIR;
                        break;
                    case 'f':       /* fold upper and lower   */
                        option |= FOLD;
                        break;
                    case 'n':       /* numeric sort           */
                        option |= NUMERIC;
                        break;
                    case 'r':       /* sort in decr. order    */
                        option |= DECR;
                        break;
                    default:
                        printf("sort: illegal option %c\n", c);
                        error("Usage: sort -dfnr [+pos1] [-pos2]"
                        break;
                    }
            else if (c == '-')
                pos2 = atoi(argv[0]+1);
            else if ((pos1 = atoi(argv[0]+1)) < 0)
                error("Usage: sort -dfnr [+pos1] [-pos2]");
        }
        if (argc || pos1 > pos2)
            error("Usage: sort -dfnr [+pos1] [-pos2]");
}
```

   The source file numcmp.c:

```
#include   <math.h>
#include   <ctype.h>
#include   <string.h>
```

```
#define    MAXSTR    100

void substr(char *s, char *t, int maxstr);

/* numcmp: compare s1 and s2 numerically                      */
int numcmp(char *s1, char *s2)
{
    double v1, v2;
    char str[MAXSTR];

    substr(s1, str, MAXSTR);
    v1 = atof(str);
    substr(s2, str, MAXSTR);
    v2 = atof(str);
    if (v1 < v2)
        return -1;
    else if (v1 > v2)
        return 1;
    else
        return 0;
}


#define    FOLD    4      /* fold upper and lower cases    */
#define    DIR     8      /* directory order               */

/* charcmp: return <0 if s<t, 0 if s==t, >0 if s>t          */
int charcmp(char *s, char *t)
{
    char a, b;
    int i, j, endpos;
    extern char option;
    extern int pos1, pos2;
    int fold = (option & FOLD) ? 1 : 0;
    int dir  = (option & DIR) ? 1 : 0;

    i = j = pos1;
    if (pos2 > 0)
        endpos = pos2;
    else if ((endpos = strlen(s)) > strlen(t))
        endpos = strlen(t);
    do {
        if (dir) {
            while (i < endpos && !isalnum(s[i]) &&
                    s[i] != ' ' && s[i] != '\0')
                i++;
            while (j < endpos && !isalnum(t[j]) &&
                    t[j] != ' ' && t[j] != '\0')
                j++;
        }
```

```
        if (i < endpos && j < endpos) {
             a = fold ?  tolower(s[i]) : s[i];
             i++;
             b = fold ?  tolower(t[j]) : t[j];
             j++;
             if (a == b && a == '\0')
                    return 0;
        }
    } while (a == b && i < endpos && j < endpos);
    return a - b;
}
```

The source file `substr.c`:

```
#include  <string.h>

void error(char *);

/* substr: get a substring of s and put in str          */
void substr(char *s, char *str)
{
    int i, j, len;
    extern int pos1, pos2;

    len = strlen(s);
    if (pos2 > 0 && len > pos2)
        len = pos2;
    else if (pos2 > 0 && len < pos2)
        error("substr: string too short");
    for (j = 0, i = pos1; i < len; i++, j++)
        str[j] = s[i];
    str[j] = '\0';
}
```

The framework for this solution is Exercises 5-14, 5-15, and 5-16.
The syntax of the sort command is

```
sort -dfnr [+pos1] [-pos2]
```

If you want to sort on fields within lines you can specify `pos1` and `pos2`;
the sort begins at `pos1` and ends just before `pos2`. Otherwise `pos1` and `pos2`
are equal to 0 and the entire line is the sort key.

The routine `readargs` reads the command line arguments. The `while`
loop in `readargs` is true while there are arguments and the argument is preceded
by a minus sign.

The first `if` statement

```
if (c == '-' && !isdigit(*(argv[0]+1)))
```

is true if the argument is a minus sign followed by a non-digit. The `switch` statement processes these arguments the same way as in Exercises 5-14, 5-15, and 5-16.

The next `else-if` statement

```
else if (t == '-')
```

is true only if the argument specified is the optional `-pos2`.

The final `else-if` statement processes `+pos1` and makes sure it is greater than zero.

`charcmp` is a modified version of the function in the previous exercises. This version handles fields.

`numcmp` compares numbers like the previous version but requires a new routine `substr` since `atof` does not take origin and length as arguments. It is safer to invent a new routine `substr` rather than to change the interface of a highly used function like `atof`.

The routines `swap`, `qsort`, `readlines`, and `writelines` are those used in Exercise 5-14. `error` is the function from Exercise 5-13.

Exercise 5-18: (page 126 K&R)

Make dcl recover from input errors.

```
#include  <stdio.h>
#include  <string.h>
#include  <ctype.h>

enum { NAME, PARENS, BRACKETS };
enum { NO, YES };

void dcl(void);
void dirdcl(void);
void errmsg(char *);
int gettoken(void);

extern int tokentype;       /* type of last token       */
extern char token[];        /* last token string        */
extern char name[];         /* identifier name          */
extern char out[];
extern int prevtoken;

/* dcl: parse a declarator                              */
void dcl(void)
{
    int ns;

    for (ns = 0; gettoken() == '*'; )  /* count *'s     */
        ns++;
    dirdcl();
    while (ns-- > 0)
        strcat(out, " pointer to");
}

/* dirdcl: parse a direct declaration                   */
void dirdcl(void)
{
    int type;

    if (tokentype == '(') {              /* ( dcl )      */
        dcl();
        if (tokentype != ')')
            errmsg("error: missing )\n");
    } else if (tokentype == NAME)     /* variable name   */
        strcpy(name, token);
```

```
        else
            errmsg("error: expected name or (dcl)\n");
    while ((type = gettoken()) == PARENS !! type == BRACKETS)
        if (type == PARENS)
            strcat(out, " function returning");
        else {
            strcat(out, " array");
            strcat(out, token);
            strcat(out, " of");
        }
}


/* errmsg: print error message and indicate avail. token   */
void errmsg(char *msg)
{
    printf("%s", msg);
    prevtoken = YES;
}
```

The source file gettoken.c:

```
#include   <ctype.h>
#include   <string.h>

enum { NAME, PARENS, BRACKETS };
enum { NO, YES };

extern int  tokentype;   /* type of last token             */
extern char token[];     /* last token string              */
int prevtoken = NO;      /* there is no previous token      */

/* gettoken: return next token                             */
int gettoken(void)
{
    int c, getch(void);
    void ungetch(int);
    char *p = token;

    if (prevtoken == YES) {
        prevtoken = NO;
        return tokentype;
    }
    while ((c = getch()) == ' ' !! c == '\t')
        ;
```

```
if (c == '(') {
    if ((c = getch()) == ')') {
        strcpy(token, "()");
        return tokentype = PARENS;
    } else {
        ungetch(c);
        return tokentype = '(';
    }
} else if (c == '[') {
    for (*p++ = c; (*p++ = getch()) != ']'; )
        ;
    *p = '\0';
    return tokentype = BRACKETS;
} else if (isalpha(c)) {
    for (*p++ = c; isalnum(c = getch()); )
        *p++ = c;
    *p = '\0';
    ungetch(c);
    return tokentype = NAME;
} else
    return tokentype = c;
}
```

We modified dirdcl a little because this function expects one of two tokens: a ')' after a call to dcl or a name. If it is neither of these tokens we invoke errmsg instead of printf. errmsg displays the error message and sets prevtoken to indicate to gettoken that a token is already available. gettoken has a new if statement at the beginning:

```
if (prevtoken == YES) {
    prevtoken = NO;
    return tokentype;
}
```

That is, if there is a token available do not get a new one yet.

Our modified version is not bullet-proof, but it has an improved error handling capability.

Exercise 5-19: (page 126 K&R)

Modify undcl so that it does not add redundant parentheses to declarations.

```
#include  <stdio.h>
#include  <string.h>
#include  <ctype.h>

#define   MAXTOKEN  100

enum { NAME, PARENS, BRACKETS };

void dcl(void);
void dirdcl(void);
int  gettoken(void);
int  nexttoken(void);

int  tokentype;          /* type of last token         */
char token[MAXTOKEN];    /* last token string          */
char out[1000];

/* undcl: convert word description to declaration       */
main()
{
    int type;
    char temp[MAXTOKEN];

    while (gettoken() != EOF) {
        strcpy(out, token);
        while ((type = gettoken()) != '\n')
            if (type == PARENS || type == BRACKETS)
                strcat(out, token);
            else if (type == '*') {
                if ((type = nexttoken()) == PARENS ||
                    type == BRACKETS)
                    sprintf(temp, "(*%s)", out);
                else
                    sprintf(temp, "*%s", out);
                strcpy(out, temp);
            } else if (type == NAME) {
                sprintf(temp, "%s %s", token, out);
                strcpy(out, temp);
            } else
                printf("invalid input at %s\n", token);
        printf("%s\n", out);
    }
    return 0;
}
```

```
enum { NO, YES };

int gettoken(void);

/* nexttoken: get the next token and push it back          */
int nexttoken(void)
{
    int type;
    extern int prevtoken;

    type = gettoken();
    prevtoken = YES;
    return type;
}
```

For the description "x is a pointer to char," the input to undcl is

```
x * char
```

and undcl produces

```
char (*x)
```

The parentheses are redundant. In fact, the parentheses are required only when the next token is either ( ) or [ ].

For example, "daytab is a pointer to an array of [13] int," the input for undcl is

```
daytab * [13] int
```

and undcl produces

```
int (*daytab)[13]
```

which is correct. On the other hand, "daytab is an array of [13] pointers to int," the input is

```
daytab [13] * int
```

and undcl produces

```
int (*daytab[13])
```

This time the parentheses are redundant.

We modified undcl to check if the next token is ( ) or [ ]. If it is ( ) or
[ ] the parentheses are necessary, otherwise the parentheses are redundant.
We look ahead one token before we make the decision about adding parentheses.

We created a simple function called nexttoken that invokes gettoken,
records the fact that there is a token available, and returns the token type.
gettoken is the function from Exercise 5-18 that checks if there is a token
already available before it gets a new one from the input.

The modified undcl does not produce redundant parentheses. For example, for the input

```
x * char
```

the modified undcl produces

```
char *x
```

For

```
daytab * [13] int
```

is

```
int (*daytab)[13]
```

And for

```
daytab [13] * int
```

is

```
int *daytab[13]
```

Exercise 5-20: (page 126 K&R)

Expand dcl to handle declarations with function argument types, qualifiers like const, and so on.

```
#include   <stdio.h>
#include   <string.h>
#include   <ctype.h>

enum { NAME, PARENS, BRACKETS };
enum { NO, YES };

void dcl(void);
void dirdcl(void);
void errmsg(char *);
int gettoken(void);

extern int tokentype;      /* type of last token       */
extern char token[];       /* last token string        */
extern char name[];        /* identifier name          */
extern char datatype[];    /* data type = char, int, etc.  */
extern char out[];
extern int prevtoken;

/* dcl: parse a declarator                             */
void dcl(void)
{
    int ns;

    for (ns = 0; gettoken() == '*'; )  /* count *'s    */
        ns++;
    dirdcl();
    while (ns-- > 0)
        strcat(out, " pointer to");
}

/* dirdcl: parse a direct declaration                  */
void dirdcl(void)
{
    int type;
    void parmdcl(void);

    if (tokentype == '(') {            /* ( dcl )       */
        dcl();
        if (tokentype != ')')
            errmsg("error: missing)\n");
```

```
        } else if (tokentype == NAME) {      /* variable name    */
            if (name[0] == '\0')
                strcpy(name, token);
        } else
            prevtoken = YES;
        while ((type = gettoken()) == PARENS || type == BRACKETS ||
                                                type == '(')
            if (type == PARENS)
                strcat(out, "function returning");
            else if (type == '(') {
                strcat(out, " function expecting");
                parmdcl();
                strcat(out, " and returning");
            } else {
                strcat(out, " array");
                strcat(out, token);
                strcat(out, " of");
            }
}

/* errmsg: print error message and indicate avail. token    */
void errmsg(char *msg)
{
    printf("%s", msg);
    prevtoken = YES;
}
```

The source file `parmdcl.c`:

```
#include    <stdio.h>
#include    <string.h>
#include    <stdlib.h>
#include    <ctype.h>

#define    MAXTOKEN   100

enum { NAME, PARENS, BRACKETS };
enum { NO, YES };

void dcl(void);
void errmsg(char *);
void dclspec(void);
int  typespec(void);
int  typequal(void);
int  compare(char **, char **);
```

```
int  gettoken(void);
extern int tokentype;        /* type of last token           */
extern char token[];         /* last token string            */
extern char name[];          /* identifier name              */
extern char datatype[];      /* data type = char, int, etc.  */
extern char out[];
extern int prevtoken;

/* parmdcl: parse a parameter declarator                      */
void parmdcl(void)
{
    do {
        dclspec();
    } while (tokentype == ',');
    if (tokentype != ')')
        errmsg("missing ) in parameter declaration\n");
}

/* dclspec: declaration specification                         */
void dclspec(void)
{
    char temp[MAXTOKEN];

    temp[0] = '\0';
    gettoken();
    do {
        if (tokentype != NAME) {
            prevtoken = YES;
            dcl();
        } else if (typespec() == YES) {
            strcat(temp, " ");
            strcat(temp, token);
            gettoken();
        } else if (typequal() == YES) {
            strcat(temp, " ");
            strcat(temp, token);
            gettoken();
        } else
            errmsg("unknown type in parameter list\n");
    } while (tokentype != ',' && tokentype != ')');
    strcat(out, temp);
    if (tokentype == ',')
        strcat(out, ",");
}
```

```
/* typespec: return YES if token is a type-specifier          */
int typespec(void)
{
    static char *types[] = {
            "char",
            "int",
            "void"
    };
    char *pt = token;

    if (bsearch(&pt, types, sizeof(types)/sizeof(char *),
        sizeof(char *), compare) == NULL)
        return NO;
    else
        return YES;
}


/* typequal: return YES if token is a type-qualifier          */
int typequal(void)
{
    static char *typeq[] = {
            "const",
            "volatile"
    };
    char *pt = token;

    if (bsearch(&pt, typeq, sizeof(typeq)/sizeof(char *),
        sizeof(char *), compare) == NULL)
        return NO;
    else
        return YES;
}

/* compare: compare two strings for bsearch                   */
int compare(char **s, char **t)
{
    return strcmp(*s, *t);
}
```

We expanded the grammar on page 122 K&R to include parameter declarators:

dcl: *optional *'s direct-dcl*

direct-dcl: *name*
                       (dcl)
                       direct-dcl (optional parm-dcl)
                       direct-dcl [optional size]

parm-dcl: *parm-dcl, dcl-spec dcl*

dcl-spec: *type-spec dcl-spec*
                          type-qual dcl-spec

This is an abbreviated version of the part of the grammar that describes declarations. We recognize a few type-specifiers described on page 211 K&R. For example,

```
void *(*comp)(int *, char *, int (*fnc)())
```

produces

```
comp: pointer to function expecting pointer to int, pointer
      to char, pointer to function returning int and returning
      pointer to void
```

We modified the function `dirdcl` and added the functions `parmdcl` and `dclspec`.

We use the lookahead facility we developed for Exercise 5-18. Sometimes we need to peek at a token before we decide what action to take. Sometimes we have a token available that we cannot use yet so we push it back; the next call to `gettoken`, elsewhere in the parser, retrieves that same token again and uses it.

`bsearch` is a standard library routine that performs binary search.

CHAPTER 6 **Structures**

Exercise 6-1: (page 136 K&R)

Our version of getword does not properly handle underscores, string constants, comments, or preprocessor control lines.   Write a better version.

```
#include   <stdio.h>
#include   <ctype.h>

/* getword: get next word or character from input        */
int getword(char *word, int lim)
{
    int c, d, comment(void), getch(void);
    void ungetch(int);
    char *w = word;

    while (isspace(c = getch()))
        ;
    if (c != EOF)
        *w++ = c;
    if (isalpha(c) || c == '_' || c == '#') {
        for ( ; --lim > 0; w++)
            if (!isalnum(*w = getch()) && *w != '_') {
                ungetch(*w);
                break;
            }
    } else if (c == '\'' || c == '"') {
        for ( ; --lim > 0; w++)
            if ((*w = getch()) == '\\')
                *++w = getch();
            else if (*w == c) {
                w++;
                break;
            } else if (*w == EOF)
                break;
```

151

```
    } else if (c == '/')
        if ((d = getch()) == '*')
            c = comment();
        else
            ungetch(d);
    *w = '\0';
    return c;
}

/* comment: skip over comment and return a character        */
int comment(void)
{
    int c;
    while ((c = getch()) != EOF)
        if (c == '*')
            if ((c = getch()) == '/')
                break;
            else
                ungetch(c);
    return c;
}
```

To handle underscores and preprocessor commands we changed

```
if (!alpha(c))
```

to

```
if (isalpha(c) || c == '_' || c == '#')
```

The alphanumeric characters and underscores that follow are treated as part of the word.

String constants may appear within single or double quotes. Once we detect a quote we gather characters until we find the closing quote or EOF.

We ignore comments and return the ending slash character. This part of the code is similar to Exercise 1-24.

Exercise 6-2: (page 143 K&R)

Write a program that reads a C program and prints in alphabetical order each group of variable names that are identical in the first 6 characters, but different somewhere thereafter. Don't count words within strings and comments. Make 6 a parameter that can be set from the command line.

```c
#include <stdio.h>
#include <ctype.h>
#include <string.h>
#include <stdlib.h>

struct tnode {                   /* the tree node:      */
    char *word;                  /* points to the text  */
    int match;                   /* match found         */
    struct tnode *left;          /* left child          */
    struct tnode *right;         /* right child         */
};

#define  MAXWORD  100
#define  YES      1
#define  NO       0

struct tnode *addtreex(struct tnode *, char *, int, int *);
void treeprint(struct tnode *);
int getword(char *, int);

/* print in alphabetic order each group of variable names   */
/* identical in the first num characters (default 6)        */
main(int argc, char *argv[])
{
    struct tnode *root;
    char word[MAXWORD];
    int found = NO;      /* YES if match was found        */
    int num;             /* number of the first ident. chars*/

    num = (--argc && (*++argv)[0] == '-') ? atoi(argv[0]+1) : 6;
    root = NULL;
    while (getword(word, MAXWORD) != EOF) {
        if (isalpha(word[0]) && strlen(word) >= num)
            root = addtreex(root, word, num, &found);
        found = NO;
    }
    treeprint(root);
    return 0;
}
```

```
struct tnode *talloc(void);
int compare(char *, struct tnode *, int, int *);

/* addtreex: add a node with w, at or below p               */
struct tnode *addtreex(struct tnode *p, char *w,
                  int num, int *found)
{
    int cond;

    if (p == NULL) {            /* a new word has arrived     */
        p = talloc();           /* make a new node            */
        p->word = strdup(w);
        p->match = *found;
        p->left = p->right = NULL;
    } else if ((cond = compare(w, p, num, found)) < 0)
        p->left = addtreex(p->left, w, num, found);
    else if (cond > 0)
        p->right = addtreex(p->right, w, num, found);
    return p;
}

/* compare: compare words and update p->match               */
int compare(char *s, struct tnode *p, int num, int *found)
{
    int i;
    char *t = p->word;

    for (i = 0; *s == *t; i++, s++, t++)
        if (*s == '\0')
            return 0;
    if (i >= num) {        /* identical in first num chars ?  */
        *found = YES;
        p->match = YES;
    }
    return *s - *t;
}

/* treexprint: in-order print of tree p if p->match == YES  */
void treexprint(struct tnode *p)
{
    if (p != NULL) {
        treexprint(p->left);
        if (p->match)
            printf("%s\n", p->word);
        treexprint(p->right);
    }
}
```

The program prints variable names that are identical in the first `num` characters. If the number of characters is not specified in the command line then it is set to 6:

```
num = (--argc && (*++argv)[0] == '-') ?  atoi(argv[0]+1) : 6;
```

The variable `found` is a boolean. `found` equals YES if the word is identical in `num` characters to a word in the tree and equals NO otherwise.

The program places a word in the tree if its first character is alphabetic and its length is greater than or equal to `num`. `getword` is the function from Exercise 6-1. The routine `addtreex`, which is a modification of `addtree` (page 141 K&R), installs a word in the tree.

The routine `compare` compares the word being placed in the tree to a word already in the tree. If there is a match in the first `num` characters, then `*found` and the match member (`p->match`) corresponding to the word in the tree are set equal to YES.

```
if (i >= num) {
     *found = YES;
     p->match = YES;
}
```

The routine `treexprint` prints the words in the tree that are identical, in the first `num` characters, to at least one other word.

Exercise 6-3: (page 143 K&R)

Write a cross-referencer that prints a list of all words in a document, and, for
each word, a list of the line numbers on which it occurs.   Remove noise words
like "the," "and," and so on.

```
#include    <stdio.h>
#include    <string.h>
#include    <ctype.h>
#include    <stdlib.h>

#define    MAXWORD    100

struct linklist {          /* linked list of line numbers    */
      int lnum;
      struct linklist *ptr;
};

struct tnode {                    /* the tree node:           */
      char *word;                 /* points to the text       */
      struct linklist *lines;     /* line numbers             */
      struct tnode *left;         /* left child               */
      struct tnode *right;        /* right child              */
};

struct tnode *addtreex(struct tnode *, char *, int);
int getword(char *, int);
int noiseword(char *);
void treexprint(struct tnode *);

/* cross-referencer                                           */
main()
{
      struct tnode *root;
      char word[MAXWORD];
      int linenum = 1;

      root = NULL;
      while (getword(word, MAXWORD) != EOF)
          if (isalpha(word[0]) && noiseword(word) == -1)
              root = addtreex(root, word, linenum);
          else if (word[0] == '\n')
              linenum++;
      treexprint(root);
      return 0;
}
```

```
struct tnode *talloc(void);
struct linklist *lalloc(void);
void addln(struct tnode *, int);

/* addtreex: add a node with w, at or below p                  */
struct tnode *addtreex(struct tnode *p, char *w, int linenum)
{
    int cond;

    if (p == NULL) {              /* a new word has arrived    */
        p = talloc();             /* make a new word           */
        p->word = strdup(w);
        p->lines = lalloc();
        p->lines->lnum = linenum;
        p->lines->ptr = NULL;
        p->left = p->right = NULL;
    } else if ((cond = strcmp(w, p->word)) == 0)
        addln(p, linenum);
    else if (cond < 0)
        p->left = addtreex(p->left, w, linenum);
    else
        p->right = addtreex(p->right, w, linenum);
    return p;
}

/* addln: add a line number to the linked list                 */
void addln(struct tnode *p, int linenum)
{
    struct linklist *temp;

    temp = p->lines;
    while (temp->ptr != NULL && temp->lnum != linenum)
        temp = temp->ptr;
    if (temp->lnum != linenum) {
        temp->ptr = lalloc();
        temp->ptr->lnum = linenum;
        temp->ptr->ptr = NULL;
    }
}

/* treexprint: in-order print of tree p                        */
void treexprint(struct tnode *p)
{
    struct linklist *temp;
```

```
    if (p != NULL) {
        treexprint(p->left);
        printf("%10s: ", p->word);
        for (temp = p->lines; temp != NULL; temp = temp->ptr)
            printf("%4d ", temp->lnum);
        printf("\n");
        treexprint(p->right);
    }
}

/* lalloc: make a linklist node                              */
struct linklist *lalloc(void)
{
    return (struct linklist *) malloc(sizeof(struct linklist));
}

/* noiseword: identify word as a noise word                  */
int noiseword(char *w)
{
    static char *nw[] = {
        "a",
        "an",
        "and",
        "are",
        "in",
        "is",
        "of",
        "or",
        "that",
        "the",
        "this",
        "to"
    };
    int cond, mid;
    int low = 0;
    int high = sizeof(nw) / sizeof(char *) - 1;

    while (low <= high) {
        mid = (low + high) / 2;
        if ((cond = strcmp(w, nw[mid])) < 0)
            high = mid - 1;
        else if (cond > 0)
            low = mid + 1;
        else
            return mid;
    }
    return -1;
}
```

The tree contains one node per distinct word.   Each node contains

a pointer to the text of the word (`word`)
a pointer to a linked list of line numbers (`lines`)
a pointer to the left child node (`left`)
a pointer to the right child node (`right`)

Each element of the linked list of line numbers is a structure of type `linklist`.   Each structure contains a line number and a pointer to the next element in the linked list.   When there are no more elements in the list, the pointer is NULL.

The routine `addtreex` is a modified version of `addtree` (page 141 K&R). `addtreex` installs the word in the tree and installs the line number in the corresponding linked list.   If it is a new word, then the first element in the linked list gets assigned the line number:

```
p->lines->lnum = linenum;
```

If a word already is in the tree

```
((cond = strcmp(w, p->word)) == 0)
```

then the routine `addln` adds the line number to the linked list.

`addln` traverses the linked list looking for an occurrence of the same line number or NULL:

```
while (temp->ptr != NULL && temp->lnum != linenum)
    temp = temp->ptr;
```

If the line number is not in the list, the routine adds the line number at the end of the linked list:

```
if (temp->lnum != linenum) {
    temp->ptr = lalloc();
    temp->ptr->lnum = linenum;
    temp->ptr->ptr = NULL;
}
```

`treexprint` is a modified version of `treeprint` (page 142 K&R). `treexprint` prints the tree in alphabetical order.   For each word in the tree, this routine prints the word and all line numbers where the word occurs.

`noiseword` is a function that searches a word in a `static` array of noise words. If a word is not one of the noise words, then the function returns -1. You can add your own words to `nw[]` as long as you keep the array in sorted ascending ASCII order.

We modified `getword` to return `'\n'` so that we can keep track of line numbers:

```
while (isspace(c = getch()) && c != '\n')
    ;
```

Exercise 6-4: (page 143 K&R)

Write a program that prints the distinct words in its input sorted into decreasing
order of frequency of occurrence.   Precede each word by its count.

```c
#include  <stdio.h>
#include  <ctype.h>

#define   MAXWORD   100
#define   NDISTINCT 1000

struct tnode {                          /* the tree node:       */
    char *word;                         /* points to the text   */
    int count;                          /* number of occurrences */
    struct tnode *left;                 /* left child           */
    struct tnode *right;                /* right child          */
};

struct tnode *addtree(struct tnode *, char *);
int getword(char *, int);
void sortlist(void);
void treestore(struct tnode *);

struct tnode *list[NDISTINCT];      /* pointers to tree nodes*/
int ntn = 0;                        /* number of tree nodes  */

/* print distinct words sorted in decreasing order of freq. */
main()
{
    struct tnode *root;
    char word[MAXWORD];
    int i;

    root = NULL;
    while (getword(word, MAXWORD) != EOF)
        if (isalpha(word[0]))
            root = addtree(root, word);
    treestore(root);
    sortlist();
    for (i = 0; i < ntn; i++)
        printf("%2d:%20s\n", list[i]->count, list[i]->word);
    return 0;
}
```

```
/* treestore: store in list[] pointers to tree nodes         */
void treestore(struct tnode *p)
{
    if (p != NULL) {
        treestore(p->left);
        if (ntn < NDISTINCT)
            list[ntn++] = p;
        treestore(p->right);
    }
}

/* sortlist: sort list of pointers to tree nodes             */
void sortlist()
{
    int gap, i, j;
    struct tnode *temp;

    for (gap = ntn/2; gap > 0; gap /= 2)
        for (i = gap; i < ntn; i++)
            for (j = i-gap; j >= 0; j -= gap) {
                if ((list[j]->count) >= (list[j+gap]->count))
                    break;
                temp = list[j];
                list[j] = list[j+gap];
                list[j+gap] = temp;
            }
}
```

The maximum number of distinct words is NDISTINCT. The structure tnode is the one used on page 140 K&R. list is an array of pointers, where each pointer points to a structure of type tnode. The variable ntn contains the number of tree nodes.

The program reads each word and places it in the tree. The routine treestore then stores each pointer to tnode in the array list. The routine sortlist is a modification of shellsort (page 62 K&R). sortlist sorts the array list in decreasing order of frequency of occurrence.

Exercise 6-5: (page 145 K&R)

Write a function `undef` that will remove a name and definition from the table maintained by `lookup` and `install`.

```
unsigned hash(char *);

/* undef: remove a name and definition from the table       */
void undef(char *s)
{
    int h;
    struct nlist *prev, *np;

    prev = NULL;
    h = hash(s);                /* hash value of string s     */
    for (np = hashtab[h]; np != NULL; np = np->next) {
        if (strcmp(s, np->name) == 0)
            break;
        prev = np;              /* remember previous entry    */
    }
    if (np != NULL) {           /* found name                 */
        if (prev == NULL)       /* first in the hash list ?   */
            hashtab[h] = np->next;
        else                    /* elsewhere in the hash list */
            prev->next = np->next;
        free((void *) np->name);
        free((void *) np->defn);
        free((void *) np);  /* free allocated structure   */
    }
}
```

The routine `undef` looks for the string `s` in the table. When `undef` finds the string `s` it exits the loop:

```
if (strcmp(s, np->name) == 0)
    break;
```

If the string `s` is not in the table, the `for` loop terminates when the pointer `np` becomes NULL.

If `np` is not NULL there is a name and a definition to be removed from the table. An entry in `hashtab` points to the beginning of a linked list. `np` points to the entry to be removed and `prev` points to an entry preceding `np`.

When `prev` is `NULL` then `np` is the first entry in the linked list starting at `hashtab[h]`:

```
if (prev == NULL)
     hashtab[h] = np->next;
else
     prev->next = np->next;
```

After removing the `np` entry, the space allocated for the name, the definition, and the structure itself is freed (`free`, page 167 K&R):

```
free((void *) np->name);
free((void *) np->defn);
free((void *) np);
```

Exercise 6-6: (page 145 K&R)

Implement a simple version of the #define processor (i.e., no arguments)
suitable for use with C programs, based on the routines of this section.   You
may also find getch and ungetch helpful.

```c
#include   <stdio.h>
#include   <ctype.h>
#include   <string.h>

#define    MAXWORD    100

struct nlist {                   /* table entry:                      */
     struct nlist *next;         /* next entry in the chain      */
     char *name;                 /* defined name                 */
     char *defn;                 /* replacement text             */
};

void error(int, char*);
int getch(void);
void getdef(void);
int getword(char *, int);
struct nlist *install(char *, char*);
struct nlist *lookup(char *);
void skipblanks(void);
void undef(char *);
void ungetch(int);
void ungets(char *);

/* simple version of #define processor                            */
main()
{
     char w[MAXWORD];
     struct nlist *p;

     while (getword(w, MAXWORD) != EOF)
         if (strcmp(w, "#") == 0) /* beginning of direct.  */
             getdef();
         else if (!isalpha(w[0]))
             printf("%s", w);      /* cannot be defined     */
         else if ((p = lookup(w)) == NULL)
             printf("%s", w);      /* not defined           */
         else
             ungets(p->defn);      /* push definition       */
     return 0;
}
```

```
/* getdef: get definition and install it                          */
void getdef(void)
{
    int c, i;
    char def[MAXWORD], dir[MAXWORD], name[MAXWORD];

    skipblanks();
    if (!isalpha(getword(dir, MAXWORD)))
        error(dir[0],
            "getdef: expecting a directive after #");
    else if (strcmp(dir, "define") == 0) {
        skipblanks();
        if (!isalpha(getword(name, MAXWORD)))
            error(name[0],
                "getdef: non-alpha - name expected");
        else {
            skipblanks();
            for (i = 0; i < MAXWORD-1; i++)
                if ((def[i] = getch()) == EOF ||
                                        def[i] == '\n')
                    break;      /* end of definition     */
            def[i] = '\0';
            if (i <= 0)              /* no definition ?       */
                error('\n', "getdef; incomplete define");
            else                     /* install definition    */
                install(name, def);
        }
    } else if (strcmp(dir, "undef") == 0) {
        skipblanks();
        if (!isalpha(getword(name, MAXWORD)))
            error(name[0], "getdef: non-alpha in undef");
        else
            undef(name);
    } else
        error(dir[0],
            "getdef: expecting a directive after #");
}

/* error: print error message and skip the rest of the line */
void error(int c, char *s)
{
    printf("error: %s\n", s);
    while (c != EOF && c != '\n')
        c = getch();
}
```

```
/* skipblanks: skip blank and tab characters                    */
void skipblanks(void)
{
    int c;

    while ((c = getch()) == ' ' || c == '\t')
        ;
    ungetch(c);
}
```

The main program contains the body of this simple processor. Directives (define, undef) are expected to follow a # and the function getdef resolves that. If getword does not return an alphabetic character, then the word could not have been defined and the program prints the word. Otherwise the program searches for a possible definition for the word. When a definition exists, the function ungets (Exercise 4-7) pushes it back in reverse order onto the input stream.

The function getdef handles the directives:

```
#define    name        definition
#undef     name
```

The name is expected to be alphanumeric.

In a define, the loop

```
for (i = 0; i < MAXWORD-1; i++)
    if ((def[i] = getch()) == EOF ||
                            def[i] == '\n')
        break;
```

gathers the definition until it finds the end of the line or end of file. If a definition exists, getdef installs it in the table using the install function (page 145 K&R).

An undef directive causes a name to be removed from the table (Exercise 6-5).

We modified getword to return spaces so that the output resembles the input data.

Exercise 7-1: (page 153 K&R)

Write a program that converts upper case to lower case or lower case to upper, depending on the name it is invoked with, as found in `argv[0]`.

```
#include <stdio.h>
#include <string.h>
#include <ctype.h>

/* lower: converts upper case to lower case                    */
/* upper: converts lower case to upper case                    */
main(int argc, char *argv[])
{
    int c;

    if (strcmp(argv[0], "lower") == 0)
        while ((c = getchar()) != EOF)
            putchar(tolower(c));
    else
        while ((c = getchar()) != EOF)
            putchar(toupper(c));
    return 0;
}
```

When the program is invoked with the name `lower`, it converts upper case to lower case. Otherwise it converts lower case to upper.

`strcmp` returns zero when `argv[0]` is the string `lower`.

The statement

```
if (strcmp(argv[0], "lower") == 0)
```

works on UNIX because `argv[0]` is the program name as the user typed it. On some operating systems `argv[0]` is the full path where the program resides, as opposed to what the user typed.

The program uses `tolower` and `toupper` from `<ctype.h>`.

Exercise 7-2: (page 155 K&R)

Write a program that will print arbitrary input in a sensible way. As a minimum, it should print non-graphic characters in octal or hexadecimal according to local custom, and break long text lines.

```
#include  <stdio.h>
#include  <ctype.h>

#define   MAXLINE  100    /* max number of chars in one line */
#define   OCTLEN    6     /* length of an octal value        */

/* print arbitrary input in a sensible way                   */
main()
{
    int c, pos;
    int inc(int pos, int n);

    pos = 0;                     /* position in the line      */
    while ((c = getchar()) != EOF)
        if (iscntrl(c) || c == ' ') {
                                 /* non-graphic or blank      */
            pos = inc(pos, OCTLEN);
            printf(" \\%03o ", c);
                                 /* newline character ?       */
            if (c == '\n') {
                pos = 0;
                putchar('\n');
            }
        } else {                 /* graphic character         */
            pos = inc(pos, 1);
            putchar(c);
        }
    return 0;
}

/* inc: increment position counter for output                */
int inc(int pos, int n)
{
    if (pos + n < MAXLINE)
        return pos+n;
    else {
        putchar('\n');
        return n;
    }
}
```

The length of an output line is MAXLINE.   The macro iscntrl is defined
in <ctype.h>. iscntrl finds the non-graphic characters: the delete character
(octal 0177) and ordinary control characters (less than octal 040).   Blanks are
also considered non-graphic characters.   Non-graphic characters are printed in
octal (preceded by a blank and a \ and followed by a blank) using OCTLEN
positions.   A newline character resets pos:

```
if (c == '\n') {
    pos = 0;
    putchar('\n');
}
```

The function inc returns the last position used and breaks a line if there
are not n places available for output.

Exercise 7-3: (page 156 K&R)

Revise `minprintf` to handle more of the other facilities of `printf`.

```
#include   <stdio.h>
#include   <stdarg.h>
#include   <ctype.h>

#define    LOCALFMT   100

/* minprintf: minimal printf with variable argument list    */
void minprintf(char *fmt, ...)
{
    va_list ap;             /* points to each unnamed arg       */
    char *p, *sval;
    char localfmt[LOCALFMT];
    int i, ival;
    unsigned uval;
    double dval;

    va_start(ap, fmt);  /* make ap point to 1st unnamed arg*/
    for (p = fmt; *p; p++) {
        if (*p != '%') {
            putchar(*p);
            continue;
        }
        i = 0;
        localfmt[i++] = '%';            /* start local fmt   */
        while (*(p+1) && !isalpha(*(p+1)))
            localfmt[i++] = *++p;       /* collect chars     */
        localfmt[i++] = *(p+1);         /* format letter     */
        localfmt[i]   = '\0';
        switch(*++p) {                  /* format letter     */
        case 'd':
        case 'i':
            ival = va_arg(ap, int);
            printf(localfmt, ival);
            break;
        case 'x':
        case 'X':
        case 'u':
        case 'o':
            uval = va_arg(ap, unsigned);
            printf(localfmt, uval);
            break;
```

```
            case 'f':
                    dval = va_arg(ap, double);
                    printf(localfmt, dval);
                    break;
            case 's':
                    sval = va_arg(ap, char *);
                    printf(localfmt, sval);
                    break;
            default:
                    printf(localfmt);
                    break;
            }
     }
     va_end(ap);                             /* clean up        */
}
```

minprintf walks along the argument list and printf does the actual printing for the facilities supported.

To handle more of the other facilities of printf we collect in localfmt the % and any other characters until an alphabetic character—the format letter. localfmt is the format argument for printf.

Exercise 7-4: (page 159 K&R)

Write a private version of scanf analogous to minprintf from the previous section.

```
#include   <stdio.h>
#include   <stdarg.h>
#include   <ctype.h>

#define    LOCALFMT   100

/* minscanf: minimal scanf with variable argument list    */
void minscanf(char *fmt, ...)
{
    va_list ap;            /* points to each unnamed arg      */
    char *p, *sval;
    char localfmt[LOCALFMT];
    int c, i, *ival;
    unsigned *uval;
    double *dval;

    i = 0;                 /* index for localfmt array        */
    va_start(ap, fmt);     /* make ap point to 1st unnamed arg*/
    for (p = fmt; *p; p++) {
        if (*p != '%') {
            localfmt[i++] = *p;        /* collect chars       */
            continue;
        }
        localfmt[i++] = '%';           /* start format        */
        while (*(p+1) && !isalpha(*(p+1)))
            localfmt[i++] = *++p;      /* collect chars        */
        localfmt[i++] = *(p+1);        /* format letter       */
        localfmt[i]   = '\0';
        switch(*++p) {                 /* format letter       */
        case 'd':
        case 'i':
            ival = va_arg(ap, int *);
            scanf(localfmt, ival);
            break;
        case 'x':
        case 'X':
        case 'u':
        case 'o':
            uval = va_arg(ap, unsigned *);
            scanf(localfmt, uval);
            break;
```

```
        case 'f':
                dval = va_arg(ap, double *);
                scanf(localfmt, dval);
                break;
        case 's':
                sval = va_arg(ap, char *);
                scanf(localfmt, sval);
                break;
        default:
                scanf(localfmt);
                break;
        }
        i = 0;                                  /* reset index    */
    }
    va_end(ap);                                 /* clean up       */
}
```

minscanf is similar to minprintf. This function collects characters from the format string until it finds an alphabetic character after a %. That is the lo-calfmt passed to scanf along with the appropriate pointer.

The arguments to scanf are pointers: a pointer to a format string and a pointer to the variable that receives the value from scanf. We use va_arg to get the value of the pointer and copy it to a local pointer and we call scanf. scanf then reads a value into the user's variable.

Exercise 7-5: (page 159 K&R)

Rewrite the postfix calculator of Chapter 4 to use `scanf` and/or `sscanf` to do
the input and number conversion.

```
#include  <stdio.h>
#include  <ctype.h>

#define   NUMBER    '0'          /* signal that a number was found  */

/* getop: get next operator or numeric operand                      */
int getop(char s[])
{
    int c, i, rc;
    static char lastc[] = " ";

    sscanf(lastc, "%c", &c);
    lastc[0] = ' ';                     /* clear last character      */
    while ((s[0] = c) == ' ' !! c == '\t')
        if (scanf("%c", &c) == EOF)
            c = EOF;
    s[1] = '\0';
    if (!isdigit(c) && c != '.')
        return c;                       /* not a number              */
    i = 0;
    if (isdigit(c))                     /* collect integer part      */
        do {
            rc = scanf("%c", &c);
            if (!isdigit(s[++i] = c))
                break;
        } while (rc != EOF);
    if (c == '.')                       /* collect fraction part     */
        do {
            rc = scanf("%c", &c);
            if (!isdigit(s[++i] = c))
                break;
        } while (rc != EOF);
    s[i] = '\0';
    if (rc != EOF)
        lastc[0] = c;
    return NUMBER;
}
```

The function `getop` (page 78 K&R) is the only routine modified.
    One thing to remember between calls to `getop` is the character following
a number. `lastc` is a two element static array that remembers the last character
read (`sscanf` expects a string).

The call

```
sscanf(lastc, "%c", &c)
```

reads the character put in `lastc[0]`. You could use

```
c = lastc[0]
```

instead.

`scanf` returns the number of successfully matched and assigned input items (page 157 K&R). And it returns `EOF` on end of file.

We also changed the expression

```
isdigit(s[++i] = c = getch())
```

into

```
rc = scanf("%c", &c);
if (!isdigit(s[++i] = c))
    break;
```

because we have to invoke `scanf`, assign the character to the string `s`, and then test for a digit.

It is possible that `scanf` found `EOF` and consequently did not alter the variable `c`. That's why we test for

```
rc != EOF
```

`scanf` does not help improve the original `getop` when we read one character at a time with `scanf`.

Another possible solution is:

```
#include   <stdio.h>
#include   <ctype.h>

#define   NUMBER     '0'          /* signal that a number was found  */

/* getop: get next operator or numeric operand                      */
int getop(char s[])
{
    int  c, rc;
    float f;

    while ((rc = scanf("%c", &c)) != EOF)
        if ((s[0] = c) != ' ' && c != '\t')
            break;
    s[1] = '\0';
    if (rc == EOF)
        return EOF;
    else if (!isdigit(c) && c != '.')
        return c;
    ungetc(c, stdin);
    scanf("%f", &f);
    sprintf(s, "%f", f);
    return NUMBER;
}
```

We read a character at a time until we find one that is neither a blank nor a tab. The loop may also terminate due to end of file.

If the character is either a digit or a decimal point, we push it back onto the input using the library function ungetc. Then we read the number. Since getop returns the number as a floating-point value, we use sprintf to convert the value of f into a character string in s.

Exercise 7-6: (page 165 K&R)

Write a program to compare two files, printing the first line where they differ.

```
#include   <stdio.h>
#include   <stdlib.h>
#include   <string.h>

#define   MAXLINE   100

/* comp: compare two files, printing first different line      */
main(int argc, char *argv[])
{
    FILE *fp1, *fp2;
    void filecomp(FILE *fp1, FILE *fp2);

    if (argc != 3) {      /* incorrect number of arguments ?     */
        fprintf(stderr, "comp: need two file names\n");
        exit(1);
    } else {
        if ((fp1 = fopen(*++argv, "r")) == NULL) {
            fprintf(stderr, "comp: can't open %s\n", *argv);
            exit(1);
        } else if ((fp2 = fopen(*++argv, "r")) == NULL) {
            fprintf(stderr, "comp: can't open %s\n", *argv);
            exit(1);
        } else {          /* found and opened files to be compared*/
            filecomp(fp1, fp2);
            fclose(fp1);
            fclose(fp2);
            exit(0);
        }
    }
}
```

```
/* filecomp: compare two files - a line at a time              */
void filecomp(FILE *fp1, FILE *fp2)
{
    char line1[MAXLINE], line2[MAXLINE];
    char *lp1, *lp2;

    do {
        lp1 = fgets(line1, MAXLINE, fp1);
        lp2 = fgets(line2, MAXLINE, fp2);
        if (lp1 == line1 && lp2 == line2) {
            if (strcmp(line1, line2) != 0) {
                printf("first difference in line\n%s\n", line1);
                lp1 = lp2 = NULL;
            }
        } else if (lp1 != line1 && lp2 == line2)
            printf("end of first file at line\n%s\n", line2);
        else if (lp1 == line1 && lp2 != line2)
            printf("end of second file at line\n%s\n", line1);
    } while (lp1 == line1 && lp2 == line2);
}
```

The number of arguments should be three: program name and two file names. The program opens the files and filecomp compares them a line at a time.

filecomp reads a line from each file. The function fgets returns a pointer to the line read or NULL on end of file. If lp1 and lp2 point to their respective lines, neither file has ended and linecomp compares the two lines. When the lines do not match, filecomp prints the line where they differ.

If lp1 or lp2 does not point to its respective line, one of the files has ended (EOF) and the files differ.

If both lp1 and lp2 do not point to their respective lines, both files have ended (EOF) and the files do not differ.

Exercise 7-7: (page 165 K&R)

Modify the pattern-finding program of Chapter 5 to take its input from a set of named files or, if no files are named as arguments, from the standard input. Should the file name be printed when a matching line is found?

```
#include   <stdio.h>
#include   <string.h>
#include   <stdlib.h>

#define    MAXLINE   1000        /* maximum input line length  */

/* find: print lines that match pattern from 1st argument   */
main(int argc, char *argv[])
{
    char pattern[MAXLINE];
    int c, except = 0, number = 0;
    FILE *fp;
    void fpat(FILE *fp, char *fname, char *pattern,
        int except, int number);

    while (--argc > 0 && (*++argv)[0] == '-')
        while (c = *++argv[0])
            switch (c) {
            case 'x':
                except = 1;
                break;
            case 'n':
                number = 1;
                break;
            default:
                printf("find: illegal option %c\n", c);
                argc = 0;
                break;
            }
    if (argc >= 1)
        strcpy(pattern, *argv);
    else {
        printf("Usage: find [-x] [-n] pattern [file ...]\n");
        exit(1);
    }
```

```
        if (argc == 1)                /* read standard input        */
            fpat(stdin, "", pattern, except, number);
        else
            while (--argc > 0)  /* get a named file                 */
                if ((fp = fopen(*++argv, "r")) == NULL) {
                    fprintf(stderr, "find: can't open %s\n",
                            *argv);
                    exit(1);
                } else {             /* named file has been opened */
                    fpat(fp, *argv, pattern, except, number);
                    fclose(fp);
                }
        return 0;
}

/* fpat: find pattern                                               */
void fpat(FILE *fp, char *fname, char *pattern,
          int except, int number)
{
        char line[MAXLINE];
        long lineno = 0;

        while (fgets(line, MAXLINE, fp) != NULL) {
            ++lineno;
            if ((strstr(line, pattern) != NULL) != except) {
                if (*fname)                     /* have a file name */
                    printf("%s - ", fname);
                if (number)                     /* print line number*/
                    printf("%ld: ", lineno);
                printf("%s", line);
            }
        }
}
```

The main program processes the optional arguments as in Chapter 5 (page 117 K&R). After that, it expects at least one more argument—the pattern. If file names do not follow the pattern, it uses the standard input. Otherwise, it opens a named file. In either case, it invokes fpat.

Most of the function fpat is similar to the code in the original main program. It reads a line at a time until fgets (page 165 K&R) returns NULL. fpat looks for the specified pattern in each line. The possibilities are:

```
(strstr(line, pattern) != NULL)   !=   except              result

0  (did not find pattern)         !=   0  (not specified)   false
1  (found pattern)                !=   0  (not specified)   true
0  (did not find pattern)         !=   1  (specified)       true
1  (found pattern)                !=   1  (specified)       false
```

When the result of that expression is true, fpat prints the file name (unless it is the standard input), the line number if it was asked for, and the line itself.

Exercise 7-8: (page 165 K&R)

Write a program to print a set of files, starting each new one on a new page, with a title and a running page count for each file.

```
#include  <stdio.h>
#include  <stdlib.h>

#define   MAXBOT    3   /* maximum # lines at bottom page   */
#define   MAXHDR    5   /* maximum # lines at head of page  */
#define   MAXLINE   100 /* maximum size of one line         */
#define   MAXPAGE   66  /* maximum # lines on one page      */

/* print: print files - each new one on a new page          */
main(int argc, char *argv[])
{
    FILE *fp;
    void fileprint(FILE *fp, char *fname);

    if (argc == 1)      /* no args; print standard input    */
        fileprint(stdin, " ");
    else                /* print file(s)                    */
        while (--argc > 0)
            if ((fp = fopen(*++argv, "r")) == NULL) {
                fprintf(stderr,
                    "print: can't open %s\n", *argv);
                exit(1);
            } else {
                fileprint(fp, *argv);
                fclose(fp);
            }
    return 0;
}

/* fileprint: print file fname                               */
void fileprint(FILE *fp, char *fname)
{
    int lineno, pageno = 1;
    char line[MAXLINE];
    int heading(char *fname, int pageno);
```

```
        lineno = heading(fname, pageno++);
        while (fgets(line, MAXLINE, fp) != NULL) {
            if (lineno == 1) {
                fprintf(stdout, "\f");
                lineno = heading(fname, pageno++);
            }
            fputs(line, stdout);
            if (++lineno > MAXPAGE - MAXBOT)
                lineno = 1;
        }
        fprintf(stdout, "\f");    /* page eject after the file  */
}


/*heading: put heading and enough blank lines                 */
int heading(char *fname, int pageno)
{
    int ln = 3;

    fprintf(stdout, "\n\n");
    fprintf(stdout, "%s    page %d\n", fname, pageno);
    while (ln++ < MAXHDR)
        fprintf(stdout, "\n");
    return ln;
}
```

The program is similar to cat (page 163 K&R).

The function fileprint takes two arguments: a pointer to an open file and a pointer to the file name (an empty string when the file is the standard input). fileprint reads and prints lines.

The character

\f

is the form feed.

The variable lineno counts the number of lines on a page. The page length is MAXPAGE. When lineno is equal to 1, fileprint puts a form feed, a new heading, and resets lineno. We also put a form feed at the end of the last page of each file.

The function heading prints the file name and page number then puts enough newline characters so that there are MAXHDR lines at the top of the page.

MAXBOT is the number of blank lines at the bottom of the page.

Exercise 7-9: (page 168 K&R)

Functions like isupper can be implemented to save space or to save time. Explore both possibilities.

```
/* isupper: return 1 (true) if c is an upper case letter    */
int isupper(char c)
{
    if (c >= 'A' && c <= 'Z')
        return 1;
    else
        return 0;
}
```

This version of isupper is a simple if-else construction that tests a character. If the character is within the range of the ASCII upper case letters it returns 1 (true), otherwise it returns 0 (false). This version of isupper saves space.

```
#define   isupper(c)      ((c) >= 'A' && (c) <= 'Z') ? 1 : 0
```

This version of isupper saves time and uses more space.

It saves time because there is no overhead of the function call and it uses more space because the macro is expanded in line every time it is invoked.

Another thing to keep in mind is the potential problem if the argument is evaluated twice.

For example,

```
char *p = "This is a string";

if (isupper(*p++))
     ...
```

The macro expands into

```
((*p++) >= 'A' && (*p++) <= 'Z') ? 1 : 0
```

which, depending on the value of *p, will increment the pointer p twice. Note that this second increment will not happen when isupper is a function because the argument to the function is evaluated once.

Normally this unexpected second increment of the pointer p leads to incorrect results.   One possible solution is

```
char *p = "This is a string";

if (isupper(*p))
      ...
p++;
```

You have to be aware of macros that may evaluate the argument more
than once.   Examples are the macros toupper and tolower in <ctype.h>.

CHAPTER 8   **The UNIX System Interface**

Exercise 8-1: (page 174 K&R)

Rewrite the program cat from Chapter 7 using read, write, open, and close instead of their standard library equivalents. Perform experiments to determine the relative speeds of the two versions.

```
#include   <stdio.h>
#include   <fcntl.h>
#include   "syscalls.h"

void error(char *fmt, ...);

/* cat: concatenate files - read / write / open / close    */
main(int argc, char *argv[])
{
    int fd;
    void filecopy(int ifd, int ofd);

    if (argc == 1)      /* no args; copy standard input    */
        filecopy(0, 1);
    else
        while (--argc > 0)
            if ((fd = open(*++argv, O_RDONLY)) == -1)
                error("cat: can't open %s", *argv);
            else {
                filecopy(fd, 1);
                close(fd);
            }
    return 0;
}
```

```
/* filecopy: copy file ifd to file ofd                        */
void filecopy(int ifd, int ofd)
{
    int n;
    char buf[BUFSIZ];

    while ((n = read(ifd, buf, BUFSIZ)) > 0)
        if (write(ofd, buf, n) != n)
            error("cat: write error");
}
```

The statement

```
if ((fd = open(*++argv, O_RDONLY)) == -1)
```

opens a file for reading and returns a file descriptor (an integer); it returns a
−1 if an error occurs.

The function `filecopy` reads `BUFSIZ` characters using the file descriptor
`ifd`. `read` returns a byte count of the characters actually read. While the
byte count is greater than 0 there are no errors; a 0 indicates end of file and a
−1 indicates an error. The function `write` writes n bytes, otherwise an error
has occurred.

`error` is the function on page 174 K&R.

This version is about twice as fast as the original version in Chapter 7 K&R.

Exercise 8-2: (page 178 K&R)

Rewrite `fopen` and `_fillbuf` with fields instead of explicit bit operations. Compare code size and execution speed.

```
#include  <fcntl.h>
#include  "syscalls.h"
#define   PERMS     0666      /* RW for owner, group, others  */

/* fopen: open file, return file ptr                          */
FILE *fopen(char *name, char *mode)
{
    int fd;
    FILE *fp;

    if (*mode != 'r' && *mode != 'w' && *mode != 'a')
        return NULL;
    for (fp = _iob; fp < _iob + OPEN_MAX; fp++)
        if (fp->flag.is_read == 0 && fp->flag.is_write == 0)
            break;                    /* found free slot       */
    if (fp >= _iob + OPEN_MAX)
        return NULL;                  /* no free slots         */

    if (*mode == 'w')                 /* create file           */
        fd = creat(name, PERMS);
    else if (*mode == 'a') {
        if ((fd = open(name, O_WRONLY, 0)) == -1)
            fd = creat(name, PERMS);
        lseek(fd, 0L, 2);
    } else
        fd = open(name, O_RDONLY, 0);
    if (fd == -1)                     /* couldn't access name  */
        return NULL;
    fp->fd = fd;
    fp->cnt = 0;
    fp->base = NULL;
    fp->flag.is_unbuf = 0;
    fp->flag.is_buf = 1;
    fp->flag.is_eof = 0;
    fp->flag.is_err = 0;
    if (*mode == 'r') {               /* read                  */
        fp->flag.is_read = 1;
        fp->flag.is_write = 0;
    } else {                          /* write                 */
        fp->flag.is_read = 0;
        fp->flag.is_write = 1;
    }
    return fp;
}
```

```
/* _fillbuf: allocate and fill input buffer                        */
int _fillbuf(FILE *fp)
{
    int bufsize;

    if (fp->flag.is_read == 0 ||
        fp->flag.is_eof  == 1 ||
        fp->flag.is_err  == 1 )
          return EOF;
    bufsize = (fp->flag.is_unbuf == 1) ? 1 : BUFSIZ;
    if (fp->base == NULL)                   /* no buffer yet    */
        if ((fp->base = (char *) malloc(bufsize)) == NULL)
            return EOF;                     /* can't get buffer */
    fp->ptr = fp->base;
    fp->cnt = read(fp->fd, fp->ptr, bufsize);
    if (--fp->cnt < 0) {
        if (fp->cnt == -1)
            fp->flag.is_eof = 1;
        else
            fp->flag.is_err = 1;
        fp->cnt = 0;
        return EOF;
    }
    return (unsigned char) *fp->ptr++;
}
```

The `typedef` for `struct _iobuf` appears on page 176 K&R. One of the members of `_iobuf` is

```
int   flag;
```

The variable `flag` is redefined in terms of bit fields:

```
struct flag_field {
    unsigned is_read  : 1;
    unsigned is_write : 1;
    unsigned is_unbuf : 1;
    unsigned is_buf   : 1;
    unsigned is_eof   : 1;
    unsigned is_err   : 1;
};
```

In the statement

```
if ((fp->flag & (_READ | _WRITE)) == 0)
    break;
```

the values _READ and _WRITE are OR'ed together:

```
(_READ      !     _WRITE)
      01    !       02          octal
      01    !       10          binary
            11                  result
```

This means that the if statement is true when both lower order bits of flag are off (neither read nor write). It verifies that an entry in _iob is not being used for read or write.

Bit fields explicitly test for this condition:

```
if (fp->flag.is_read == 0 && fp->flag.is_write == 0)
     break;
```

The next modification explicitly sets the bits:

```
fp->flag.is_unbuf = 0;
fp->flag.is_buf = 1;
fp->flag.is_eof = 0;
fp->flag.is_err = 0;
```

Next,

```
fp->flag = (*mode == 'r') ? _READ : _WRITE;
```

sets flag according to mode. If it is 'r', it sets flag to _READ, otherwise it sets flag to _WRITE.

With bit fields, if the mode is 'r', the bit is_read is set to 1. If not, the is_write bit is set to 1:

```
if (*mode == 'r') {
    fp->flag.is_read = 1;
    fp->flag.is_write = 0;
} else {
    fp->flag.is_read = 0;
    fp->flag.is_write = 1;
}
```

The function _fillbuf changes similarly.
The function _fillbuf returns an EOF for the following situations: the

file was not open for reading, an end of file already happened, or an error has been detected

```
if ((fp->flag & (_READ!_EOF!_ERR)) != _READ)
```

This condition is tested with bit fields:

```
if (fp->flag.is_read == 0 !!
    fp->flag.is_eof  == 1 !!
    fp->flag.is_err  == 1)
```

Next,

```
bufsize = (fp->flag & _UNBUF) ?  1 : BUFSIZ;
```

changes to

```
bufsize = (fp->flag.is_unbuf == 1) ?  1 : BUFSIZ;
```

And

```
      fp->flag != _EOF;
else
      fp->flag != _ERR;
```

becomes

```
      fp->flag.is_eof = 1;
else
      fp->flag.is_err = 1;
```

The code size of the modified function was larger and the functions were slower. Bit fields are machine dependent and may slow down execution.

Exercise 8-3: (page 179 K&R)

Design and write _flushbuf, fflush, and fclose.

```
#include  "syscalls.h"

/* _flushbuf: allocate and flush output buffer             */
int _flushbuf(int x, FILE *fp)
{
    unsigned nc;                        /* # of chars to flush  */
    int bufsize;                        /* size of buffer alloc. */

    if (fp < _iob || fp >= _iob + OPEN_MAX)
        return EOF;                     /* error: invalid pointer*/
    if ((fp->flag & (_WRITE | _ERR)) != _WRITE)
        return EOF;
    bufsize = (fp->flag & _UNBUF) ? 1 : BUFSIZ;
    if (fp->base == NULL) {             /* no buffer yet        */
        if ((fp->base = (char *) malloc(bufsize)) == NULL) {
            fp->flag |= _ERR;
            return EOF;                 /* can't get buffer     */
        }
    } else {                            /* buffer already exists */
        nc = fp->ptr - fp->base;
        if (write(fp->fd, fp->base, nc) != nc) {
            fp->flag |= _ERR;
            return EOF;                 /* error: return EOF    */
        }
    }
    fp->ptr = fp->base;                 /* beginning of buffer  */
    *fp->ptr++ = (char) x;              /* save current char    */
    fp->cnt = bufsize - 1;
    return x;
}

/* fclose: close file                                        */
int fclose(FILE *fp)
{
    int rc;                             /* return code          */

    if ((rc = fflush(fp)) != EOF) {     /* anything to flush?   */
        free(fp->base);                 /* free allocated buffer */
        fp->ptr = NULL;
        fp->cnt = 0;
        fp->base = NULL;
        fp->flag &= ~(_READ | _WRITE);
    }
    return rc;
}
```

```
/* fflush: flush buffer associated with file fp                    */
int fflush(FILE *fp)
{
      int rc = 0;

      if (fp < _iob || fp >= _iob + OPEN_MAX)
          return EOF;                        /* error: invalid pointer*/
      if (fp->flag & _WRITE)
          rc = _flushbuf(0, fp);
      fp->ptr = fp->base;
      fp->cnt = (fp->flag & _UNBUF) ?  1  :  BUFSIZ;
      return rc;
}
```

`_flushbuf` returns an EOF if the file was not open for writing or an error has occurred:

```
if ((fp->flag & (_WRITE | _ERR)) != _WRITE)
    return EOF;
```

If there is no buffer yet, one is allocated as in `_fillbuf` (page 178 K&R). If the buffer exists, then its characters are flushed.

The next step is to save the argument in the buffer:

```
*fp->ptr++ = (char) x;
```

The number of possible characters in the buffer (`fp->cnt`) is then one less than the buffer size because of the character just saved.

The function `fclose` invokes `fflush`. If the file was opened for writing it might be necessary to flush some characters. `fclose` resets members of the `_iobuf` structure so that `fopen` will not encounter meaningless values in a free slot. The return code is 0 if no errors exist.

`fflush` checks for a valid file pointer and calls `_flushbuf` if the file was open for writing. `fflush` then resets `ptr` and `cnt`, then returns `rc`.

Exercise 8-4: (page 179 K&R)

The standard library function

```
int fseek(FILE *fp, long offset, int origin)
```

is identical to `lseek` except that `fp` is a file pointer instead of a file descriptor and the return value is an `int` status, not a position. Write `fseek`. Make sure that your `fseek` coordinates properly with the buffering done for the other functions of the library.

```
#include "syscalls.h"

/* fseek: seek with a file pointer                        */
int fseek(FILE *fp, long offset, int origin)
{
    unsigned nc;                    /* # of chars to flush     */
    long rc = 0;                    /* return code             */

    if (fp->flag & _READ) {
        if (origin == 1)            /* from current position ? */
            offset -= fp->cnt;      /* remember chars in buffer */
        rc = lseek(fp->fd, offset, origin);
        fp->cnt = 0;                /* no characters buffered  */
    } else if (fp->flag & _WRITE) {
        if ((nc = fp->ptr - fp->base) > 0)
            if (write(fp->fd, fp->base, nc) != nc)
                rc = -1;
        if (rc != -1)               /* no errors yet ?         */
            rc = lseek(fp->fd, offset, origin);
    }
    return (rc == -1) ? -1 : 0;
}
```

The variable `rc` contains the return code. It is set to -1 when an error occurs.

There are two situations in `fseek`: the file is open for reading or it is open for writing.

When the file is open for reading and the origin is 1, the offset is counted from the current position (the other cases are: origin 0, the offset is counted from the beginning of the file; origin 2, the offset is counted from the end of the file). To measure the offset from the current position, `fseek` takes into account the characters already in the buffer:

```
if (origin == 1)
    offset -= fp->cnt;
```

fseek then invokes lseek and discards the buffered characters:

```
rc = lseek(fp->fd, offset, origin);
fp->cnt = 0;
```

When the file is open for writing, fseek first flushes buffered characters if any:

```
if ((nc = fp->ptr - fp->base) > 0)
    if (write(fp->fd, fp->base, nc) != nc)
        rc = -1;
```

If there are no errors, fseek calls lseek:

```
if (rc != -1)
    rc = lseek(fp->fd, offset, origin);
```

The function fseek returns 0 for proper seeks.

Exercise 8-5: (page 184 K&R)

Modify the fsize program to print the other information contained in the inode
entry.

```
#include  <stdio.h>
#include  <string.h>
#include  <fcntl.h>              /* flags for read and write   */
#include  <sys/types.h>          /* typedefs                   */
#include  <sys/stat.h>           /* structure returned by stat */
#include  "dirent.h"

int stat(char *, struct stat *);
void dirwalk(char *, void (*fcn)(char *));

/* fsize: print inode #, mode, links, size of file "name"    */
void fsize(char *name)
{
    struct stat stbuf;

    if (stat(name, &stbuf) == -1) {
        fprintf(stderr, "fsize: can't access %s\n", name);
        return;
    }
    if ((stbuf.st_mode & S_IFMT) == S_IFDIR)
        dirwalk(name, fsize);
    printf("%5u %6o %3u %8ld %s\n", stbuf.st_ino,
        stbuf.st_mode, stbuf.st_nlink, stbuf.st_size, name);
}
```

We modified fsize to print the inode number, the file mode in octal, the
number of links to the file, the file size, and the file name. You may choose
to print more information—it depends on what is significant to you.
    The function dirwalk appears on page 182 K&R.

Exercise 8-6: (page 189 K&R)

The standard library function `calloc(n,size)` returns a pointer to `n` objects of size `size`, with the storage initialized to zero. Write `calloc`, by calling `malloc` or by modifying it.

```
#include    "syscalls.h"

/* calloc: allocate n objects of size size          */
void *calloc(unsigned n, unsigned size)
{
    unsigned i, nb;
    char *p, *q;

    nb = n * size;
    if ((p = q = malloc(nb)) != NULL)
        for (i = 0; i < nb; i++)
            *p++ = 0;
    return q;
}
```

The function `calloc` allocates `n` objects of size `size`. The total number of bytes to be allocated is `nb`:

```
nb = n * size;
```

`malloc` returns a pointer to a storage area of `nb` bytes. The pointers `p` and `q` remember the beginning of this allocated storage area. If the allocation was successful, the `nb` bytes allocated are initialized to 0:

```
for (i = 0; i < nb; i++)
    *p++ = 0;
```

`calloc` returns a pointer to the beginning of the allocated and initialized storage area.

Exercise 8-7: (page 189 K&R)

malloc accepts a size request without checking its plausibility; free believes
that the block it is asked to free contains a valid size field.   Improve these
routines so they take more pains with error checking.

```
#include  "syscalls.h"

#define   MAXBYTES  (unsigned) 10240

static unsigned maxalloc;/* max number of units allocated       */
static Header   base;    /* empty list to get started           */
static Header   *freep = NULL;     /* start of free list         */

/* malloc: general-purpose storage allocator                     */
void *malloc(unsigned nbytes)
{
      Header *p, *prevp;
      static Header *morecore(unsigned);
      unsigned nunits;

      if (nbytes > MAXBYTES) {        /* not more than MAXBYTES    */
          fprintf(stderr,
                  "alloc: can't allocate more than %u bytes\n",
                  MAXBYTES);
          return NULL;
      }
      nunits = (nbytes + sizeof(Header) - 1) / sizeof(Header) + 1;

      /* . . . */                     /* as on page 187 K&R        */
}


#define   NALLOC    1024              /* minimum #units to request */

/* morecore: ask system for more memory                          */
static Header *morecore(unsigned nu)
{
      char *cp, *sbrk(int);
      Header *up;

      if (nu < NALLOC)
          nu = NALLOC;
      cp = sbrk(nu * sizeof(Header));
      if (cp == (char *) -1)          /* no space at all           */
          return NULL;
      up = (Header *) cp;
      up->s.size = nu;
```

```
    maxalloc = (up->s.size > maxalloc) ? up->s.size : maxalloc;
    free((void *)(up+1));
    return freep;
}


/* free: put block ap in free list                              */
void free(void *ap)
{
    Header *bp, *p;

    bp = (Header *)ap - 1;          /* point to block header    */
    if (bp->s.size == 0 || bp->s.size > maxalloc) {
        fprintf(stderr, "free: can't free %u units\n",
                bp->s.size);
        return;
    }
    for (p = freep; !(bp > p && bp < p->s.ptr); p = p->s.ptr)

        /* . . . */   ;               /* as on page 188 K&R       */
}
```

The `malloc` function checks the number of bytes requested against some arbitrary constant `MAXBYTES`. Select a value for `MAXBYTES` that works best for your system.

When `morecore` allocates a new block, the `static` variable `maxalloc` remembers the size of the largest block used so far. This way the function `free` can verify that the value of size is not 0 and it is not larger than the largest block allocated.

Exercise 8-8: (page 189 K&R)

Write a routine `bfree(p,n)` that will free an arbitrary block p of n characters
into the free list maintained by `malloc` and `free`. By using `bfree`, a user can
add a static or external array to the free list at any time.

```
#include  "syscalls.h"

/* bfree: free an arbitrary block p of n chars                 */
unsigned bfree(char *p, unsigned n)
{
    Header *hp;

    if (n < sizeof(Header))
        return 0;                        /* too small to be useful   */
    hp = (Header *) p;
    hp->s.size = n / sizeof(Header);
    free((void *)(hp+1));
    return hp->s.size;
}
```

The routine `bfree` takes two arguments: a pointer p and a number of
characters n. It will free the block only if its size is at least `sizeof(Header)`,
otherwise it returns 0.
The pointer p is cast to `Header` type and assigned to `hp`:

```
hp = (Header *) p;
```

The size of the block in units of `sizeof(Header)` is:

```
hp->s.size = n / sizeof(Header);
```

The last step calls the function `free`. Since `free` expects the pointer to
be just past the header area, we use (`hp+1`), as `morecore` does, and cast it to
type (`void *`).
The routine `bfree` returns 0 if the block is too small, otherwise it returns
the size of the block in `sizeof(Header)` units.

Index